This book
belongs
to:

_____

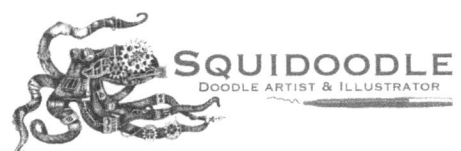

SQUIDOODLE
DOODLE ARTIST & ILLUSTRATOR

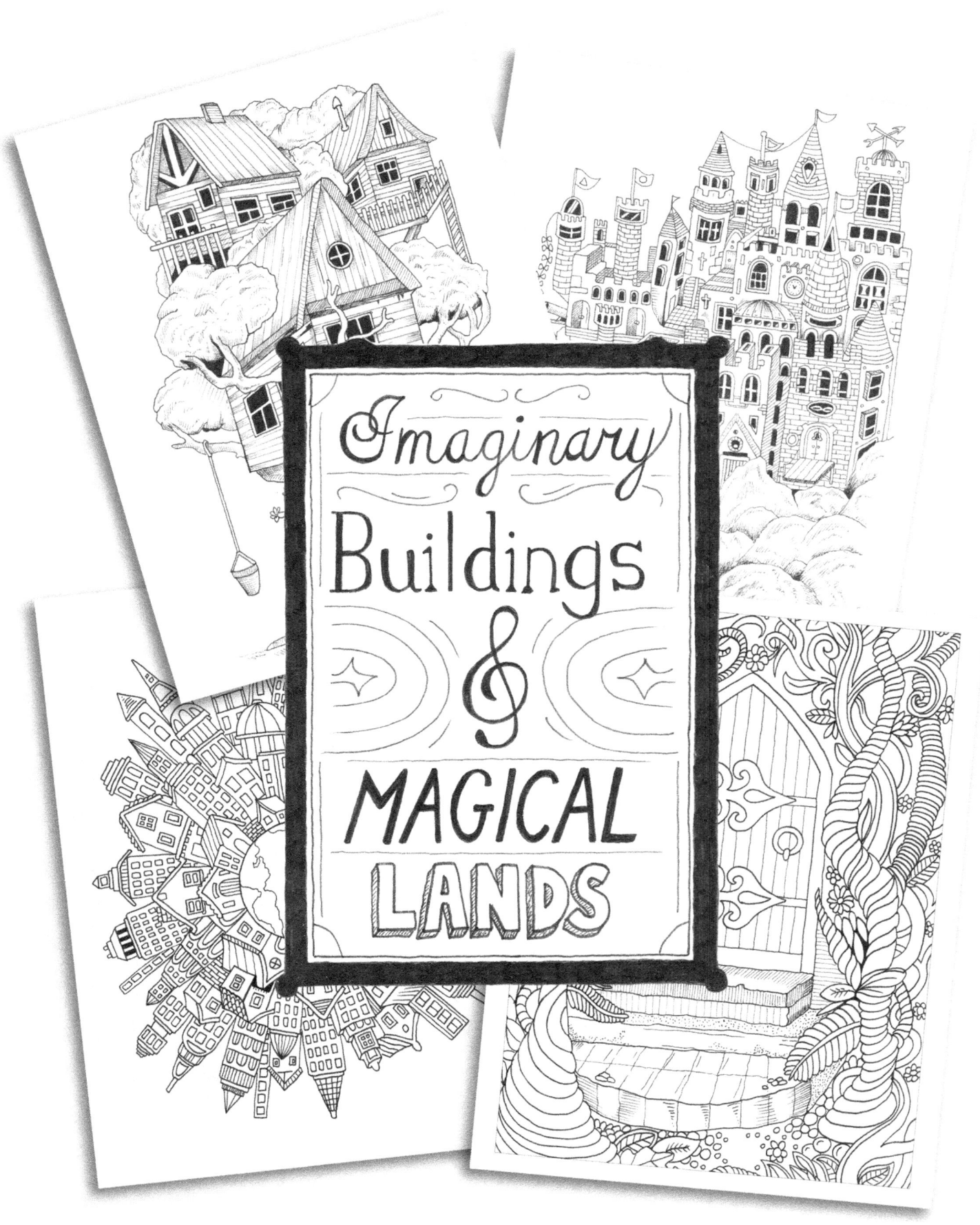

Imaginary Buildings & MAGICAL LANDS

Escape to a magical land of fantasy castles, forests, floating towns,
temples and doodled cities! Grab your pencils and pens....
the adventure starts over the page.....

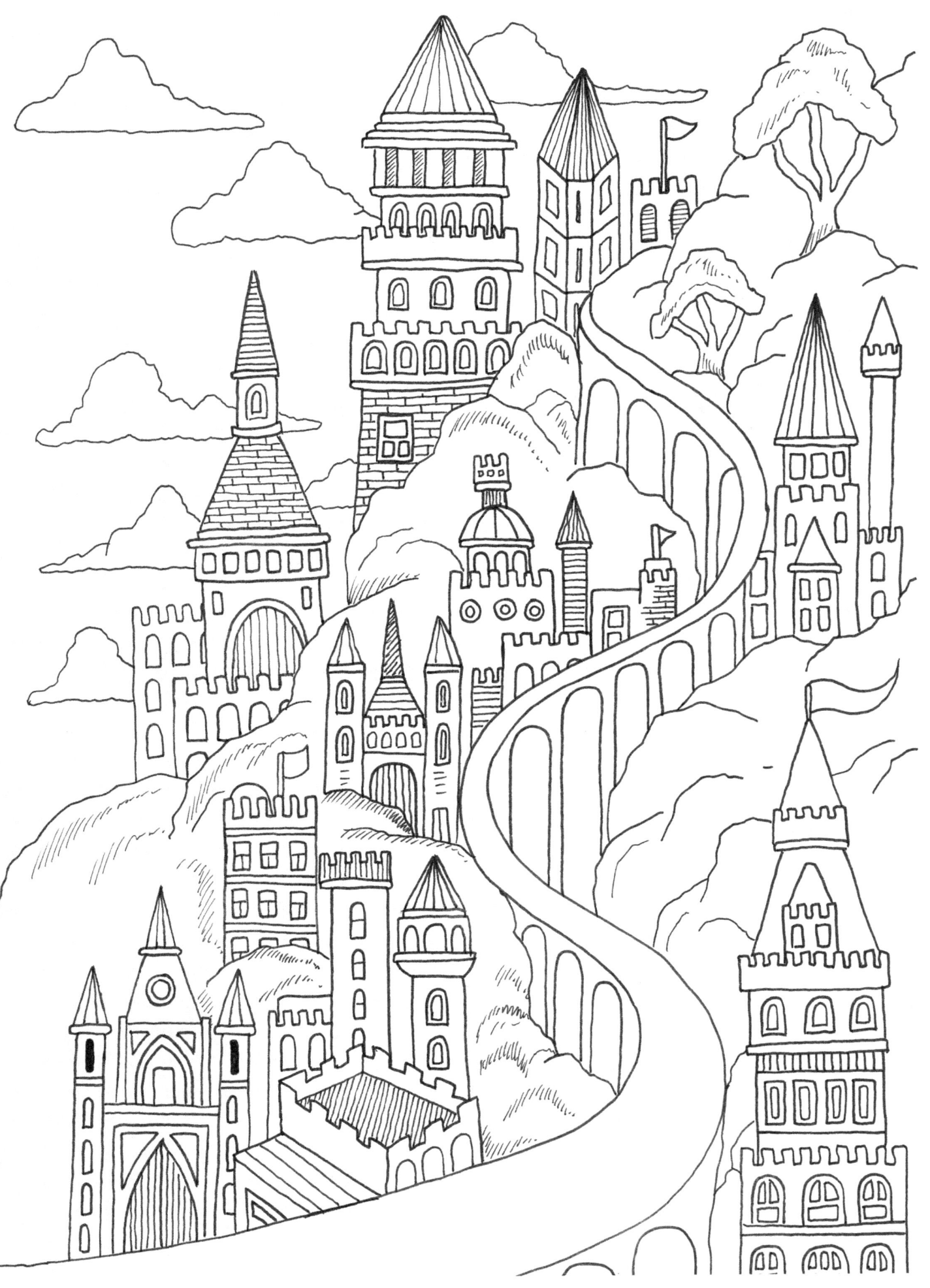

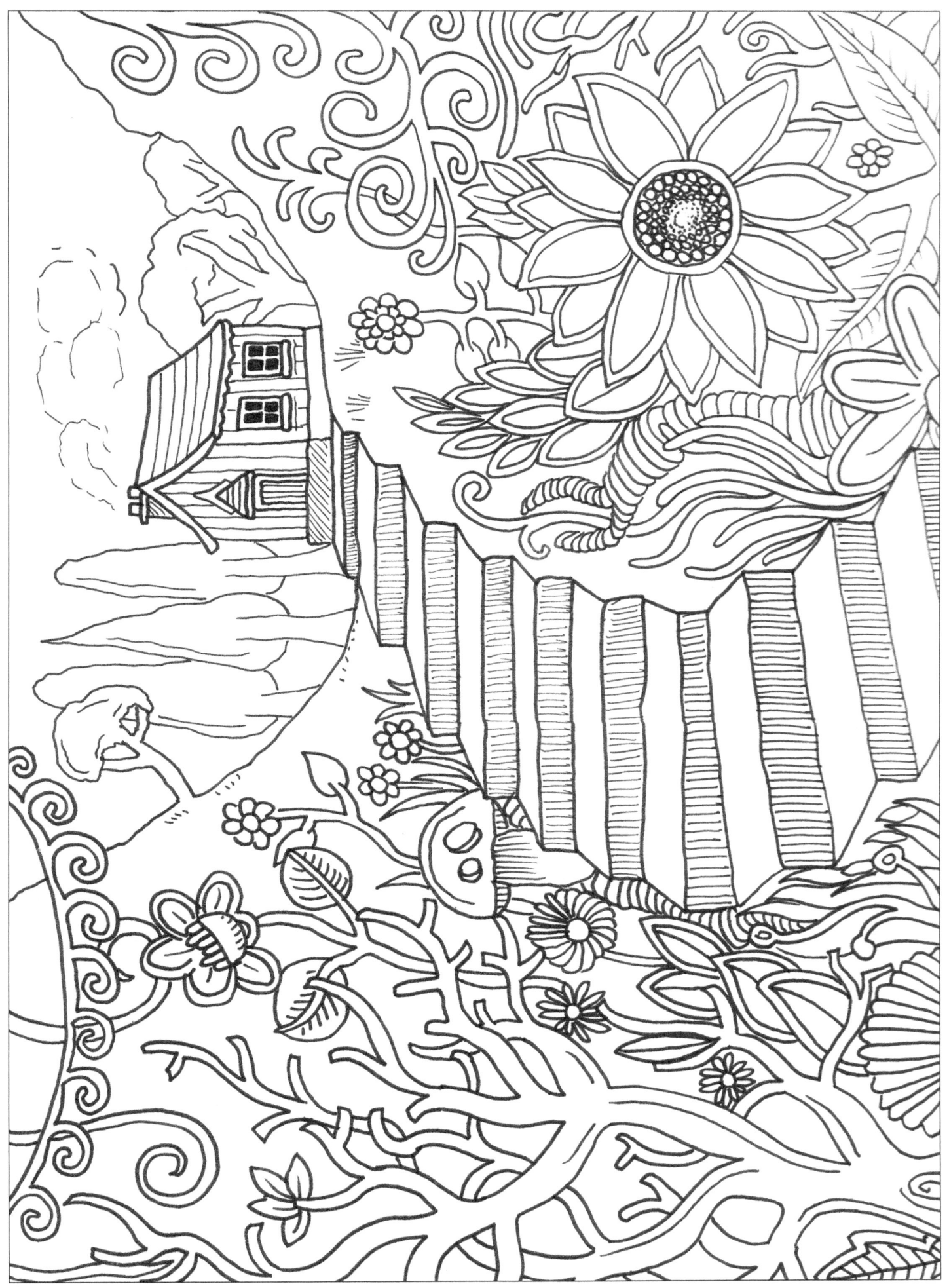

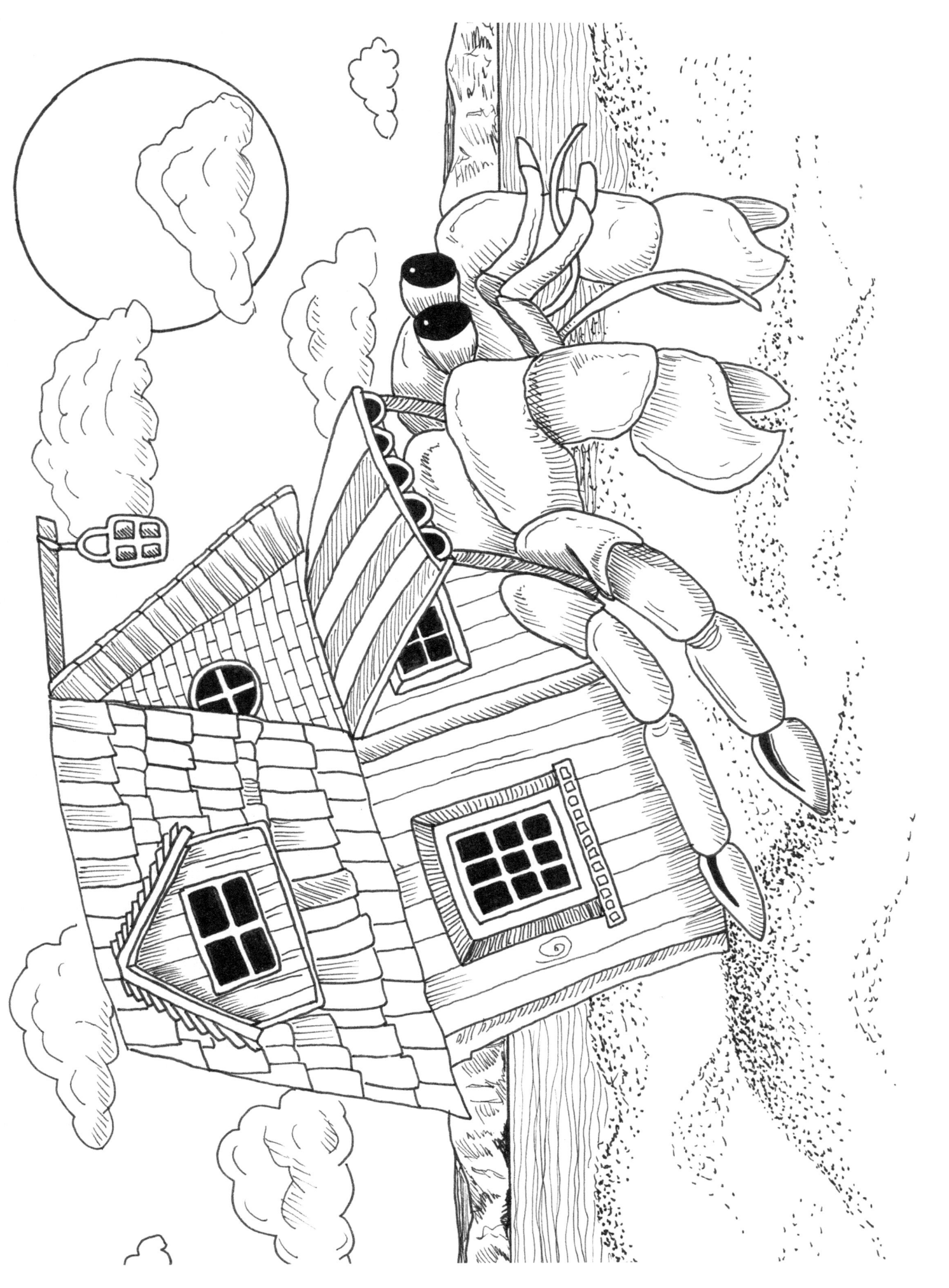

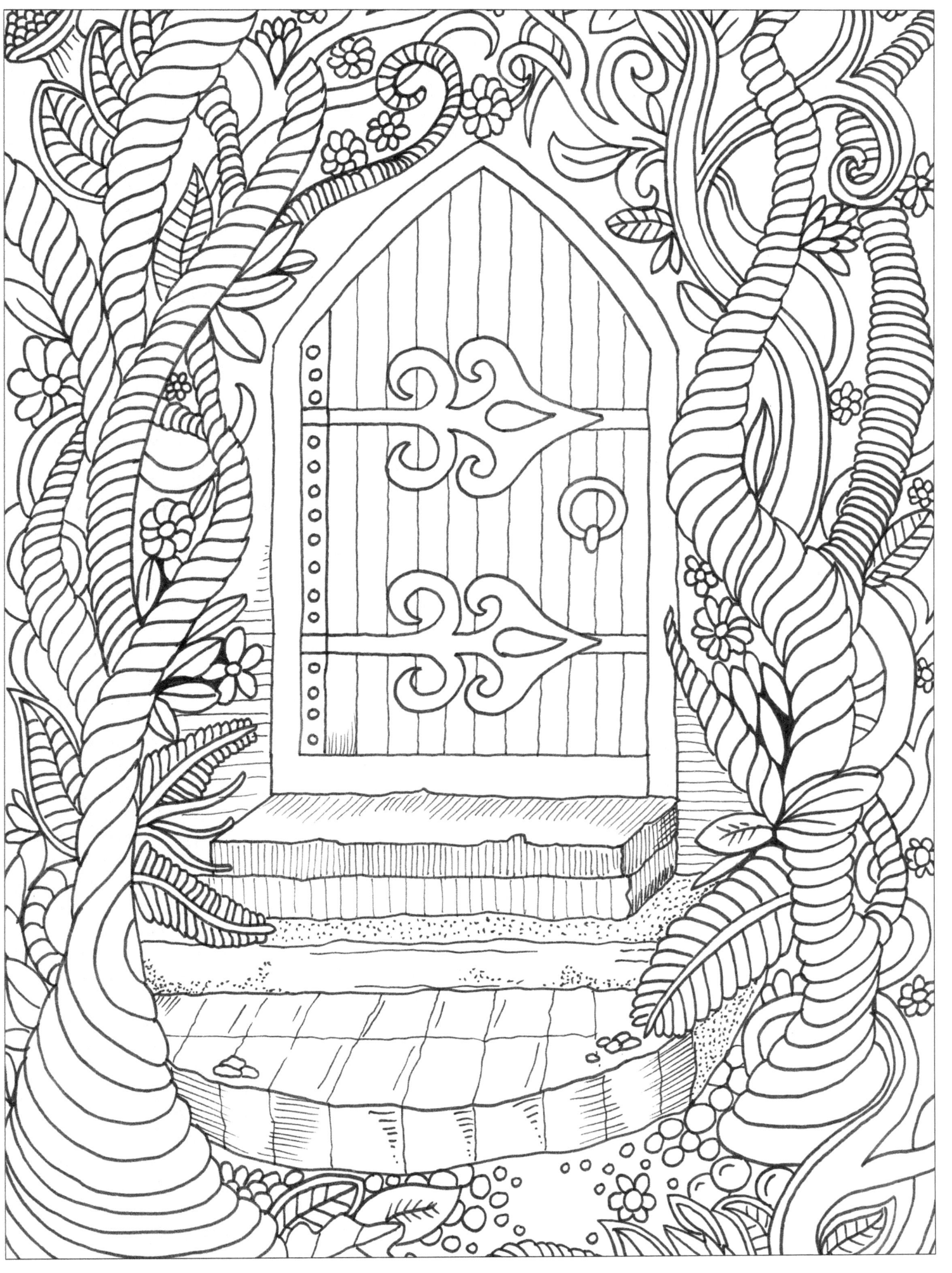

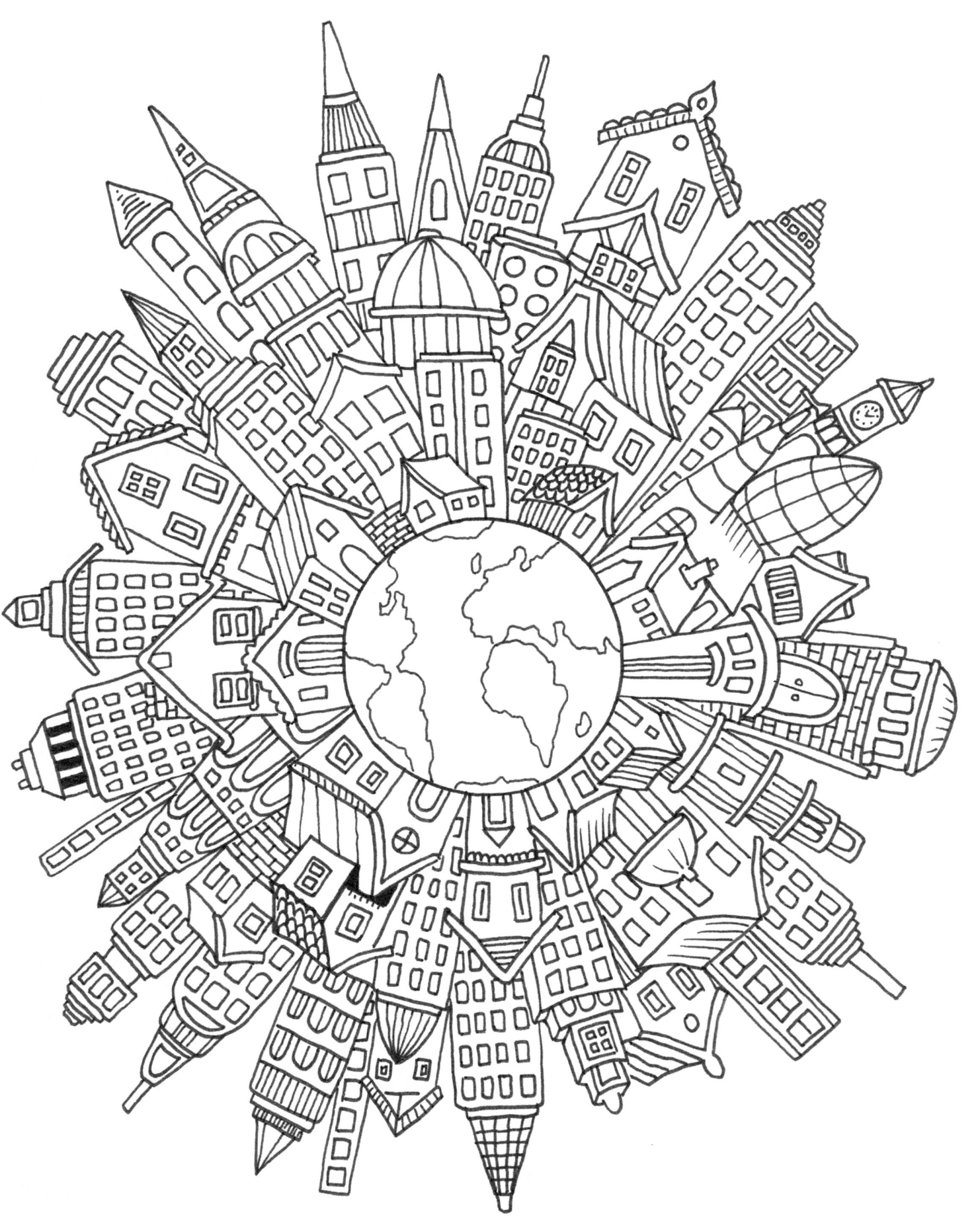

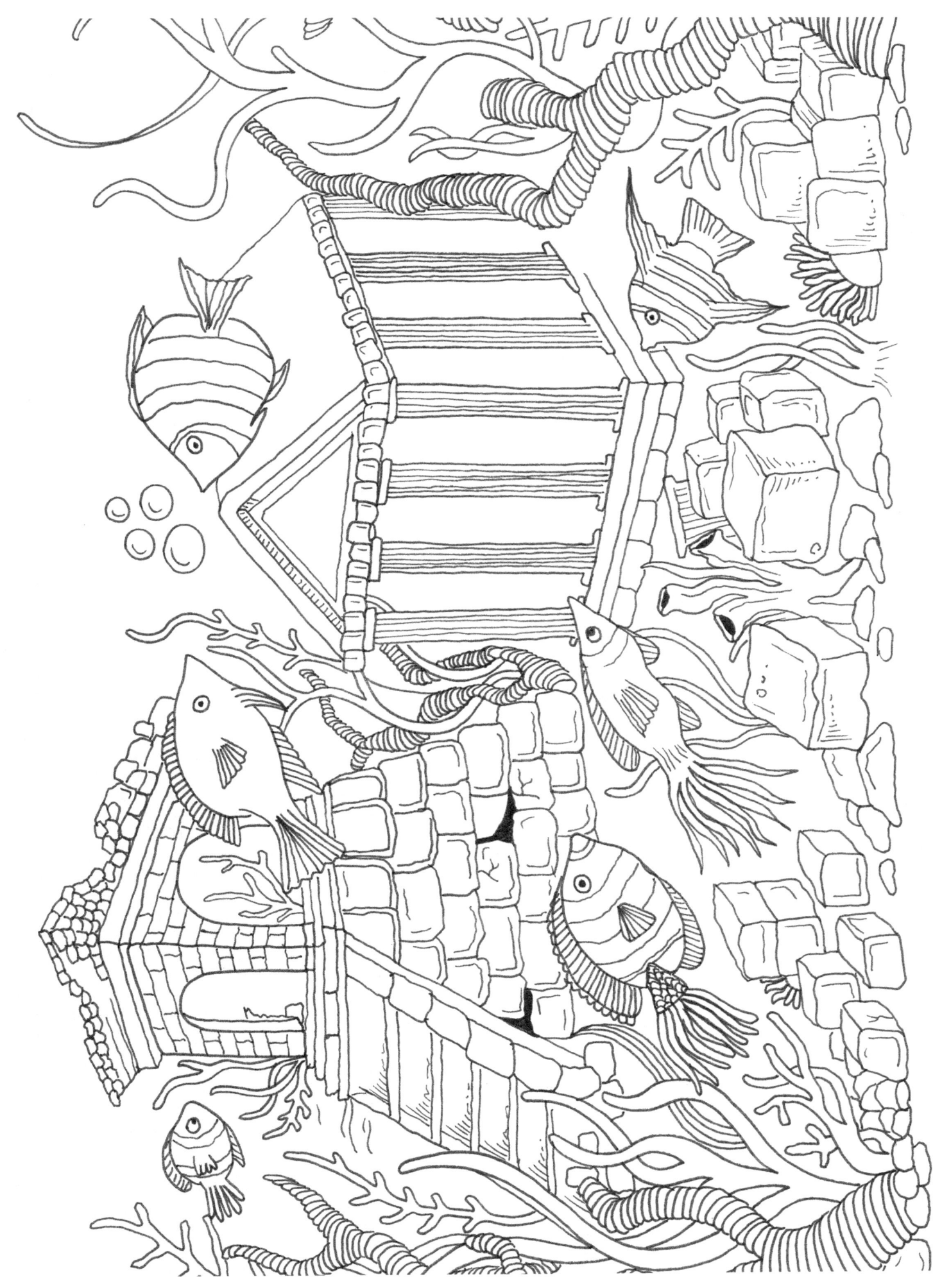

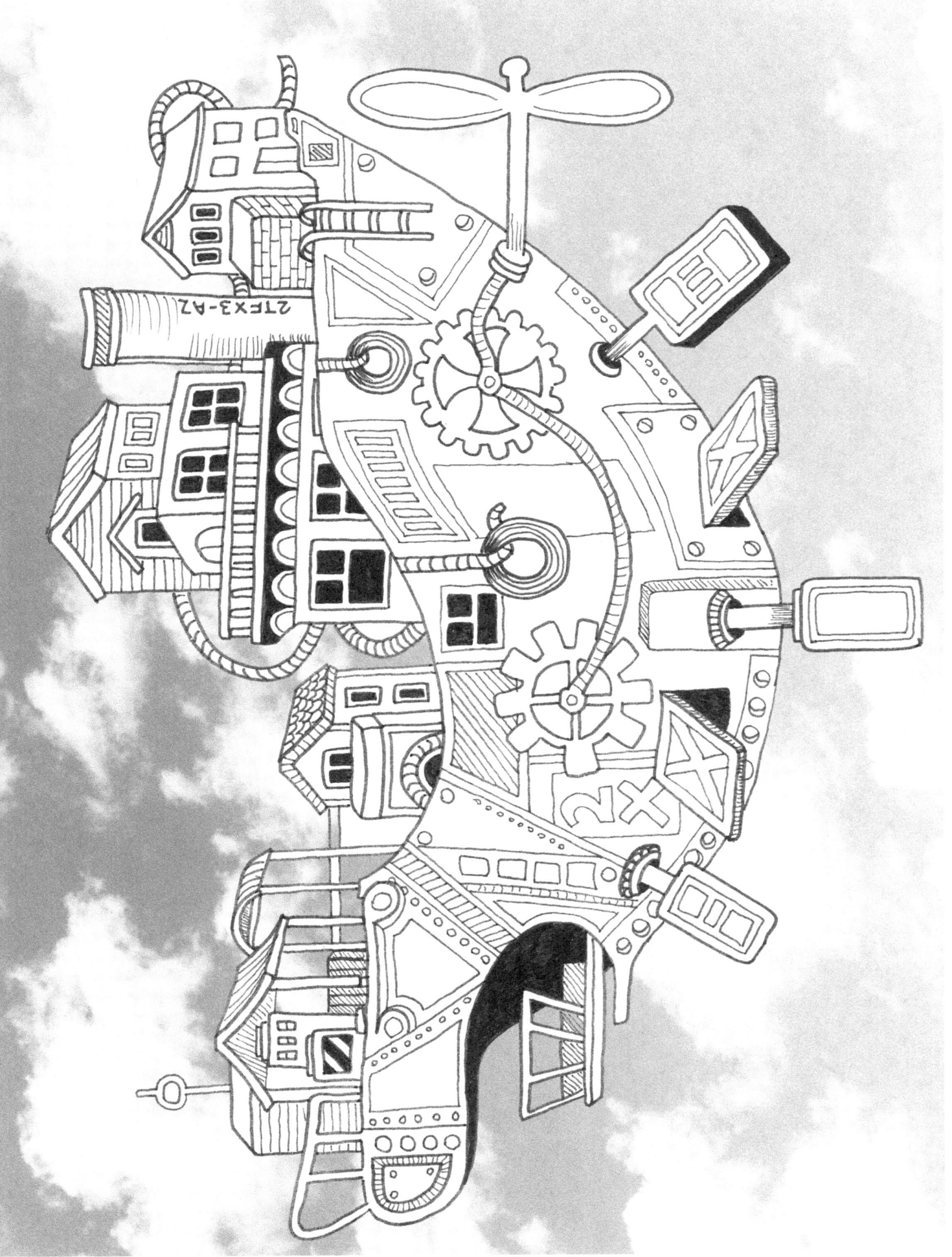

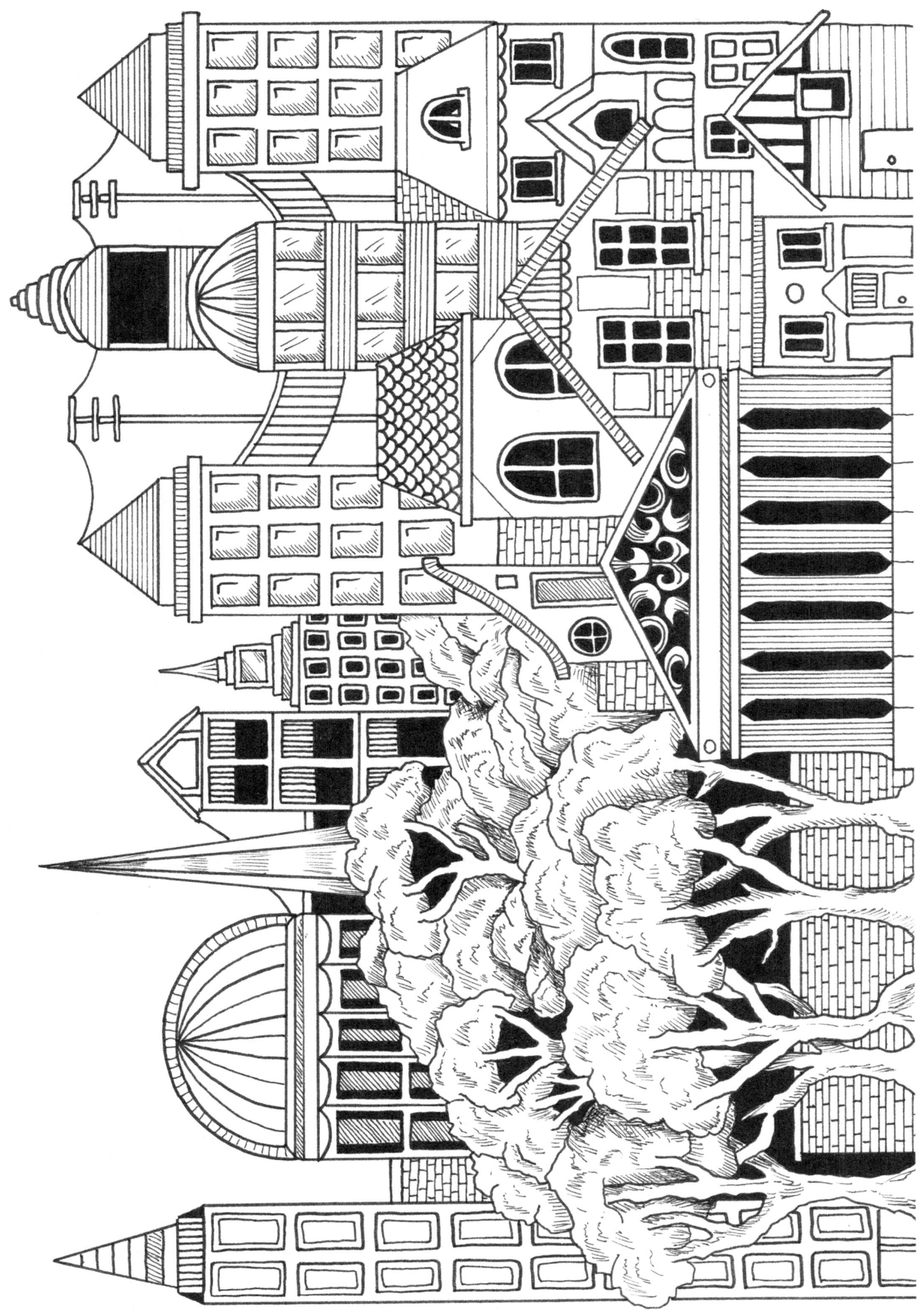

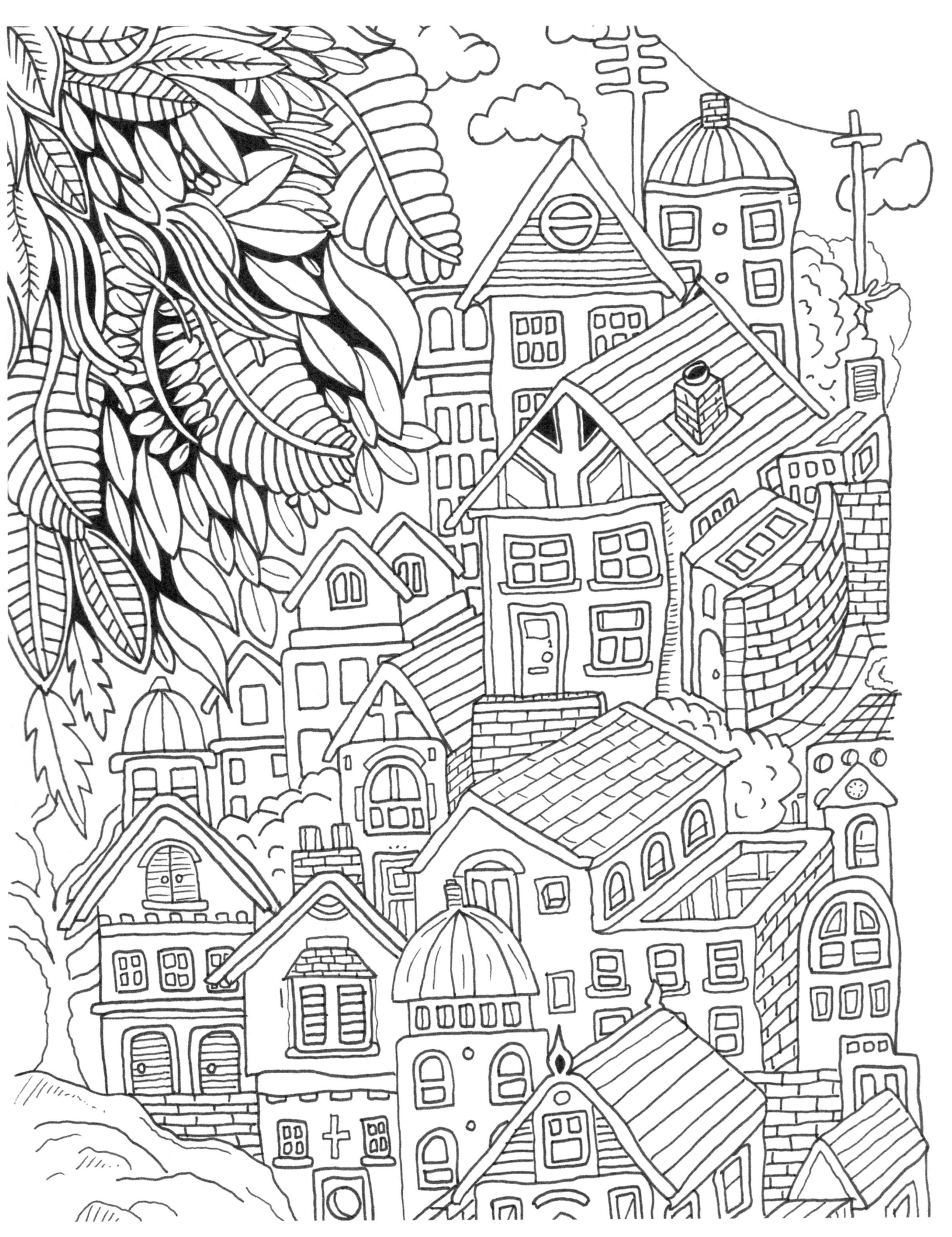

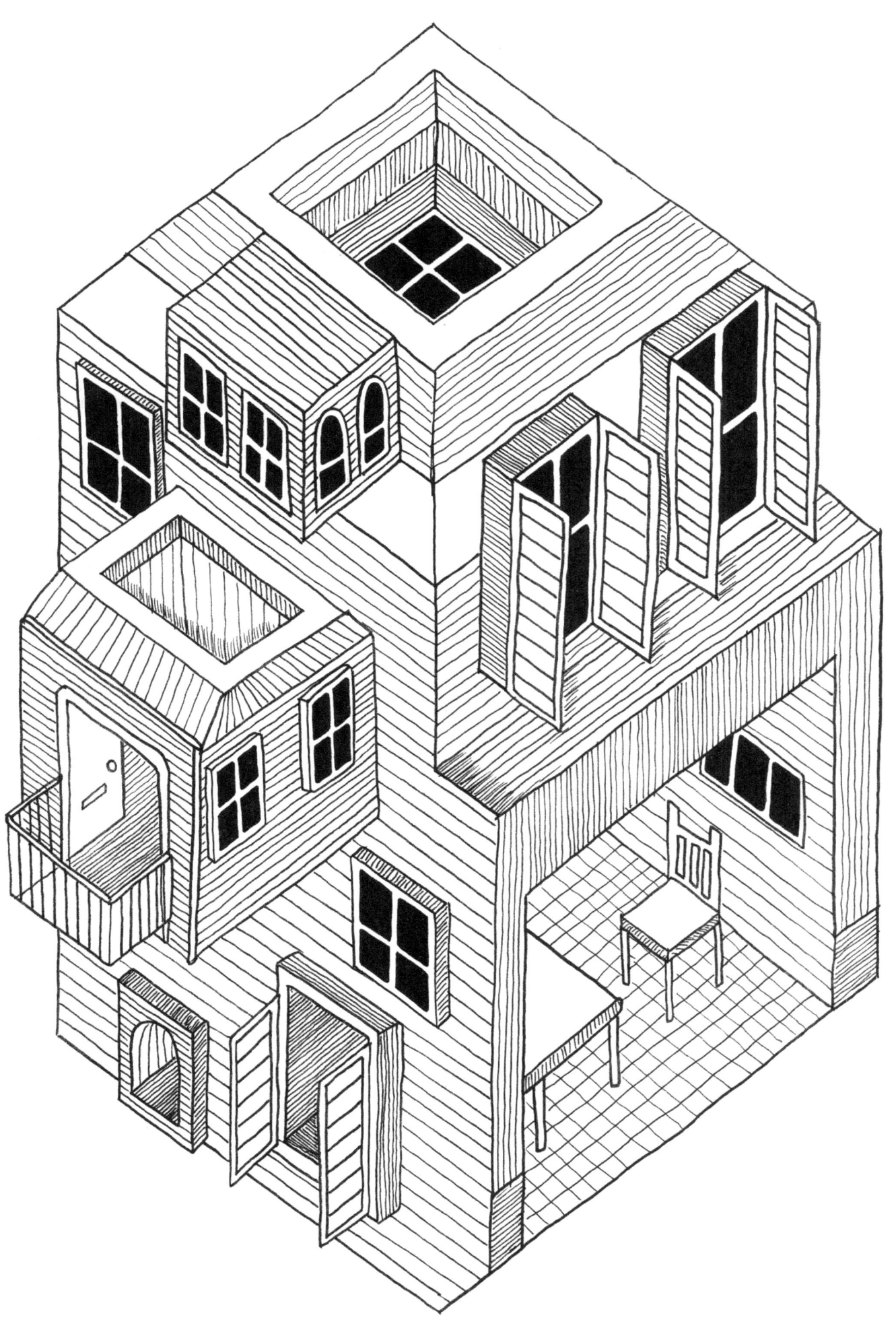

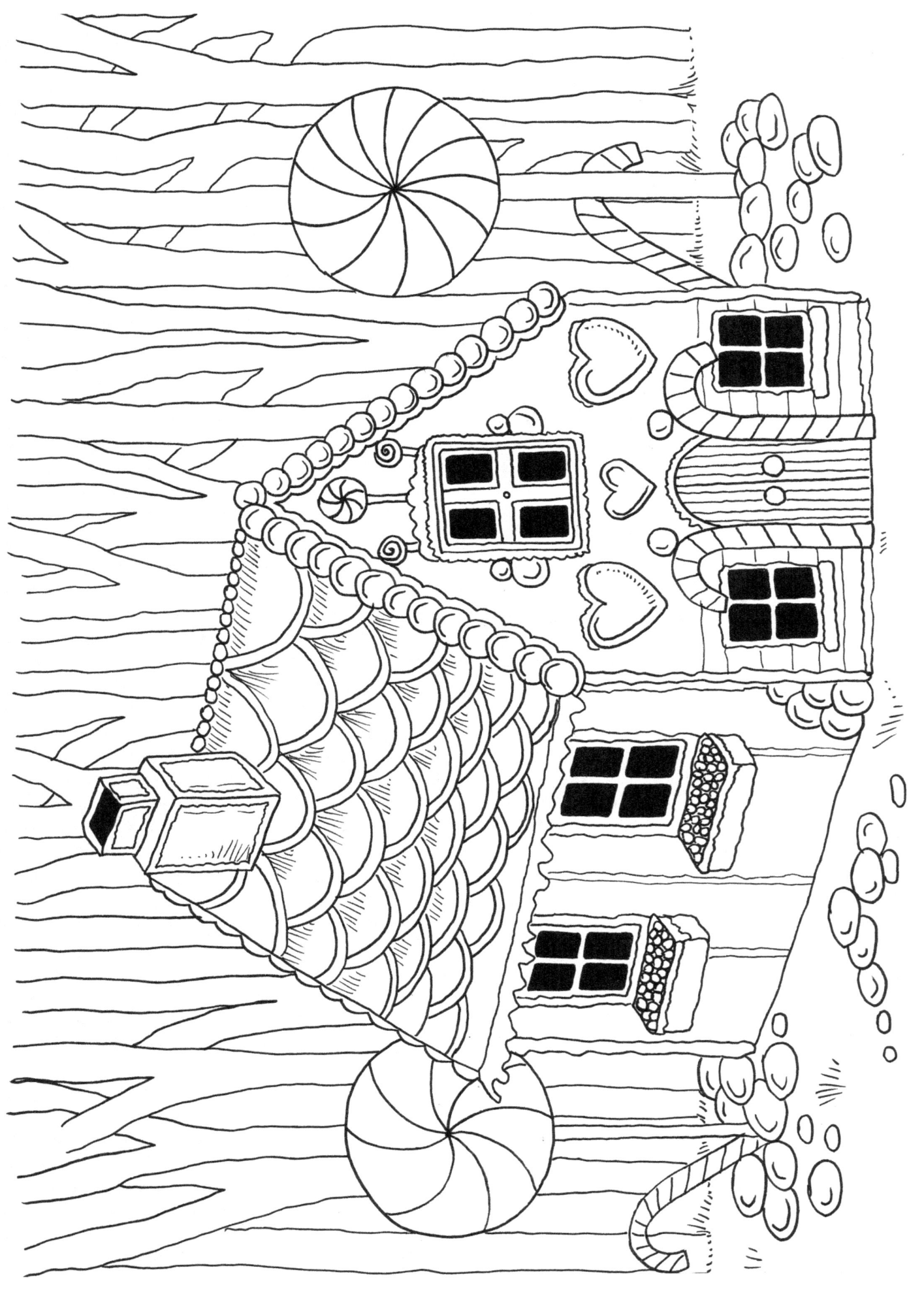

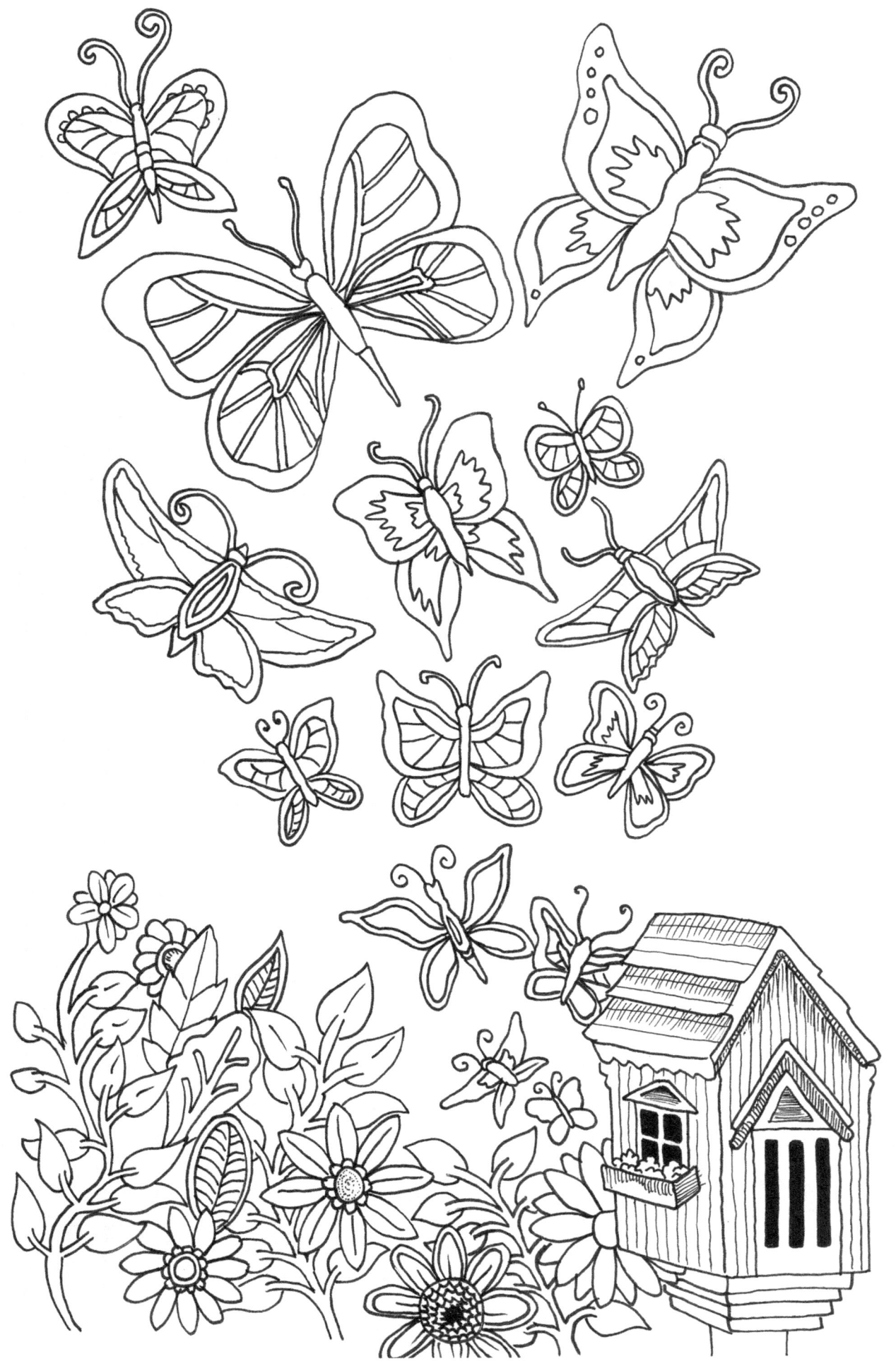

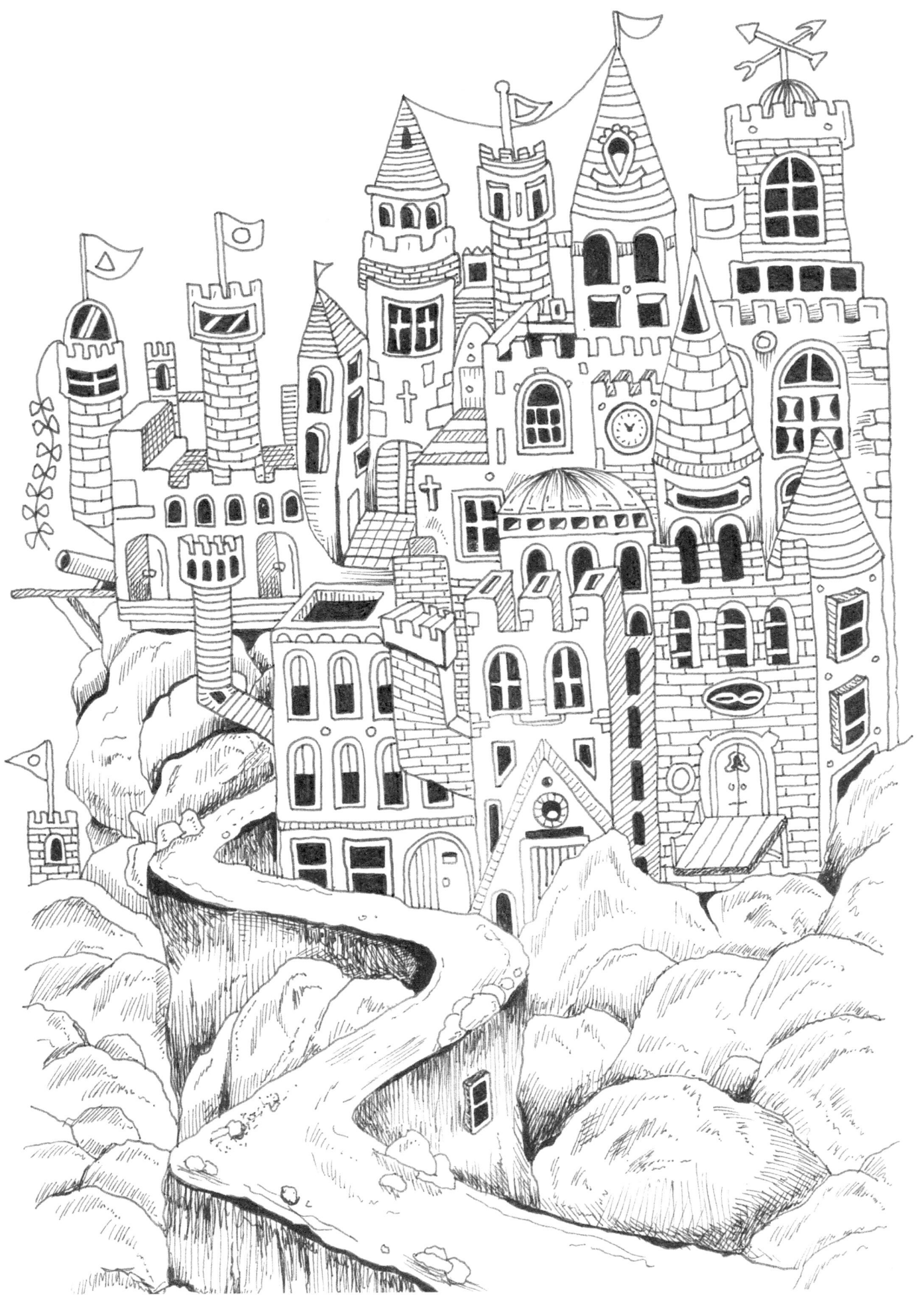

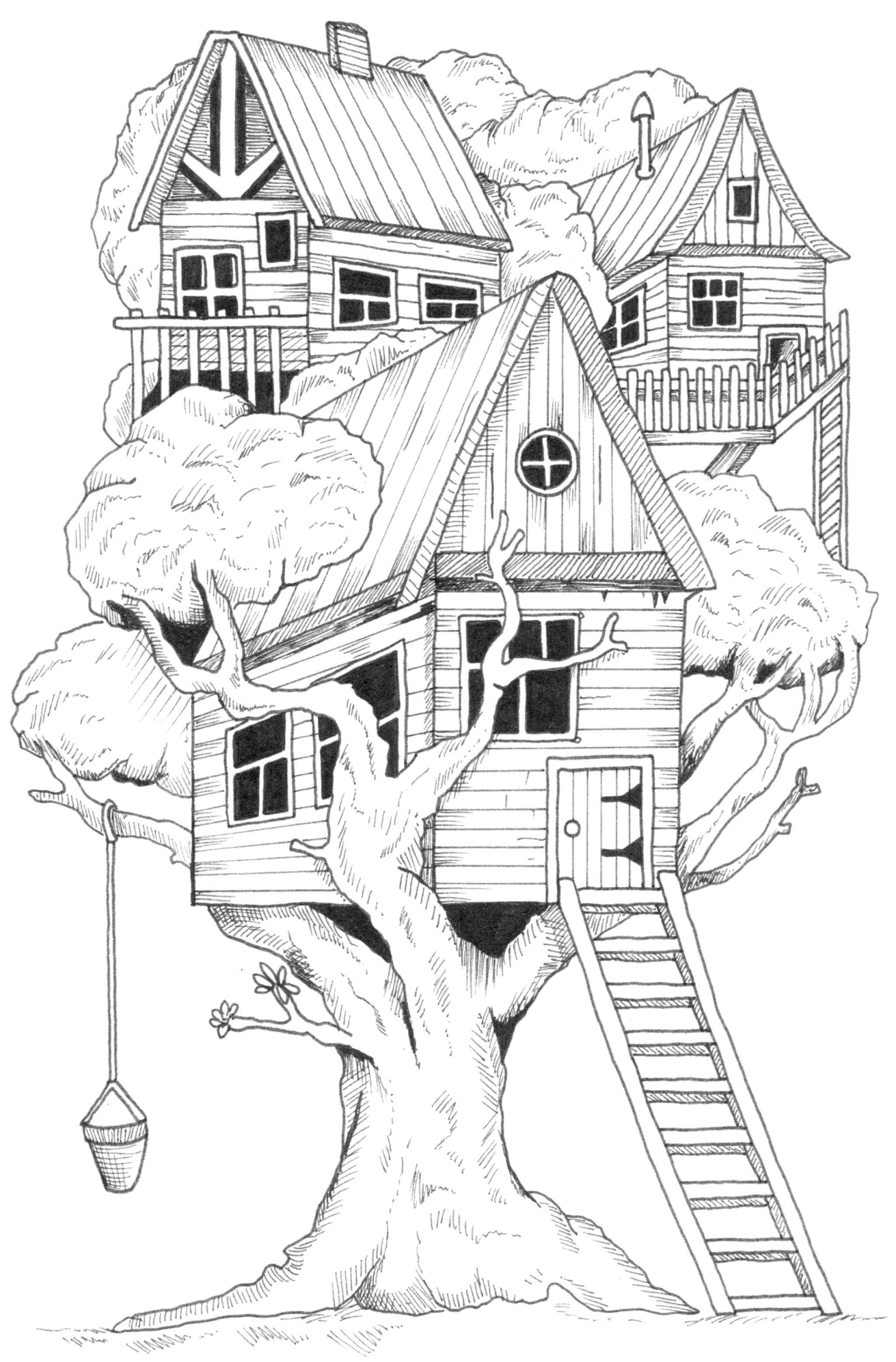

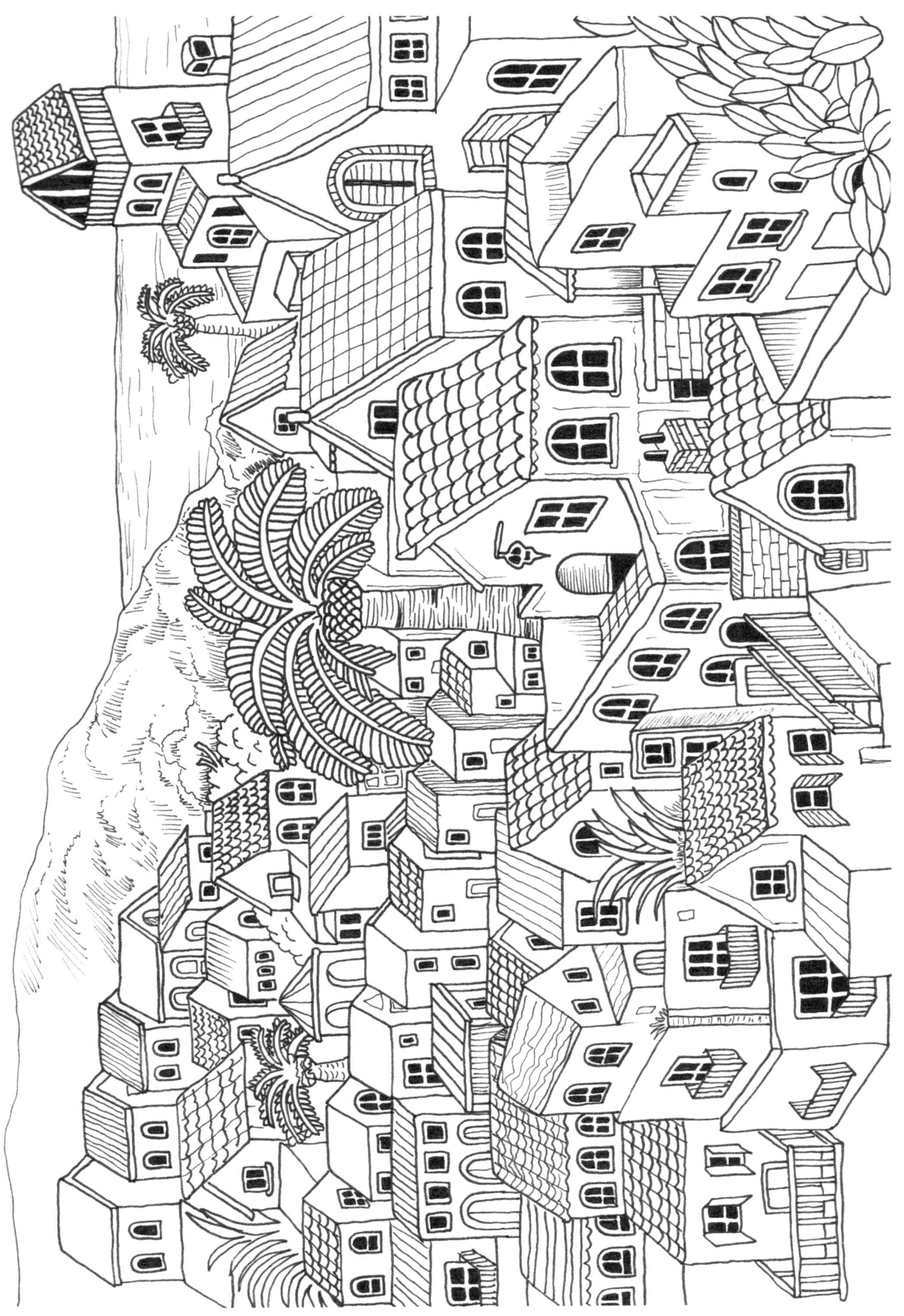

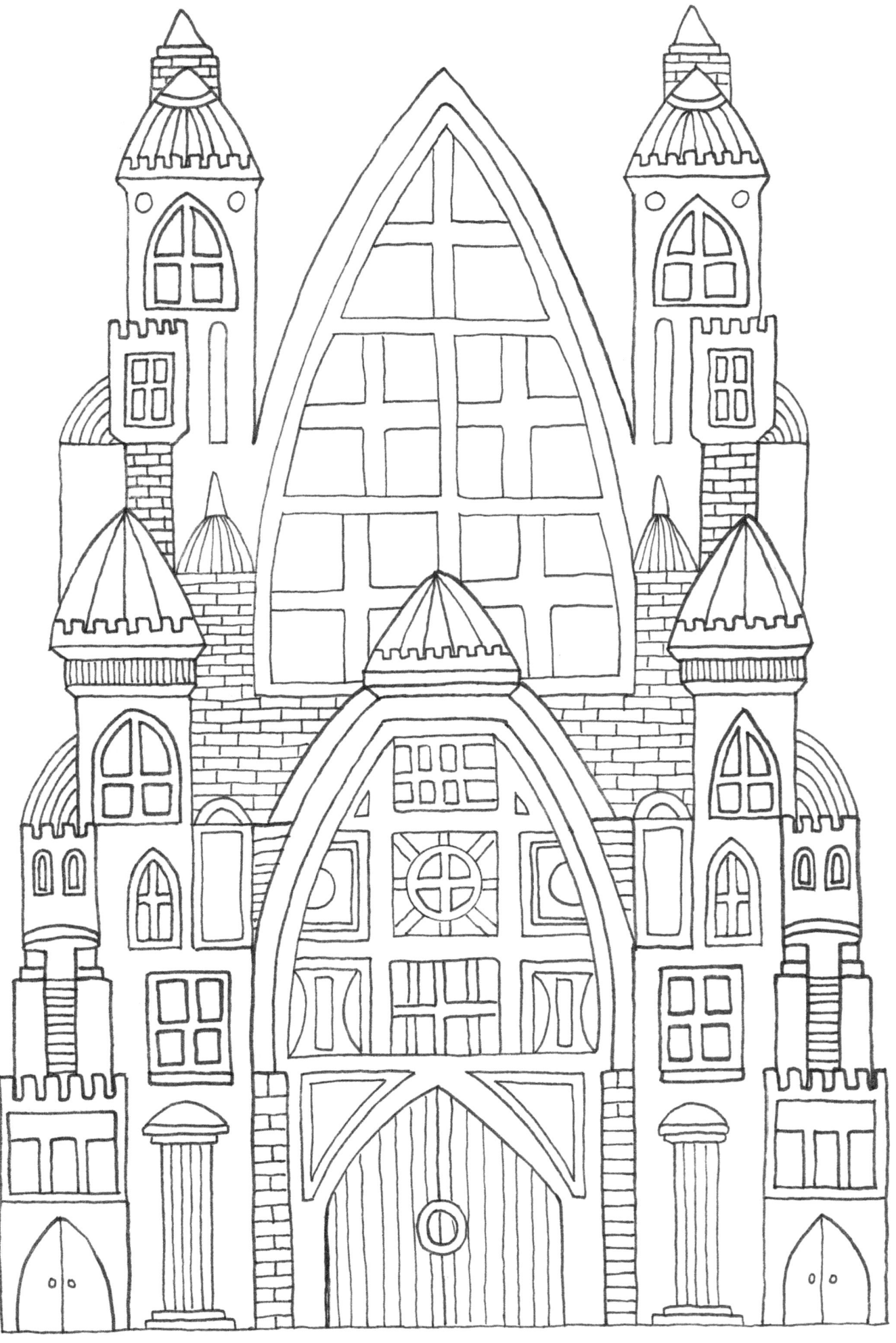

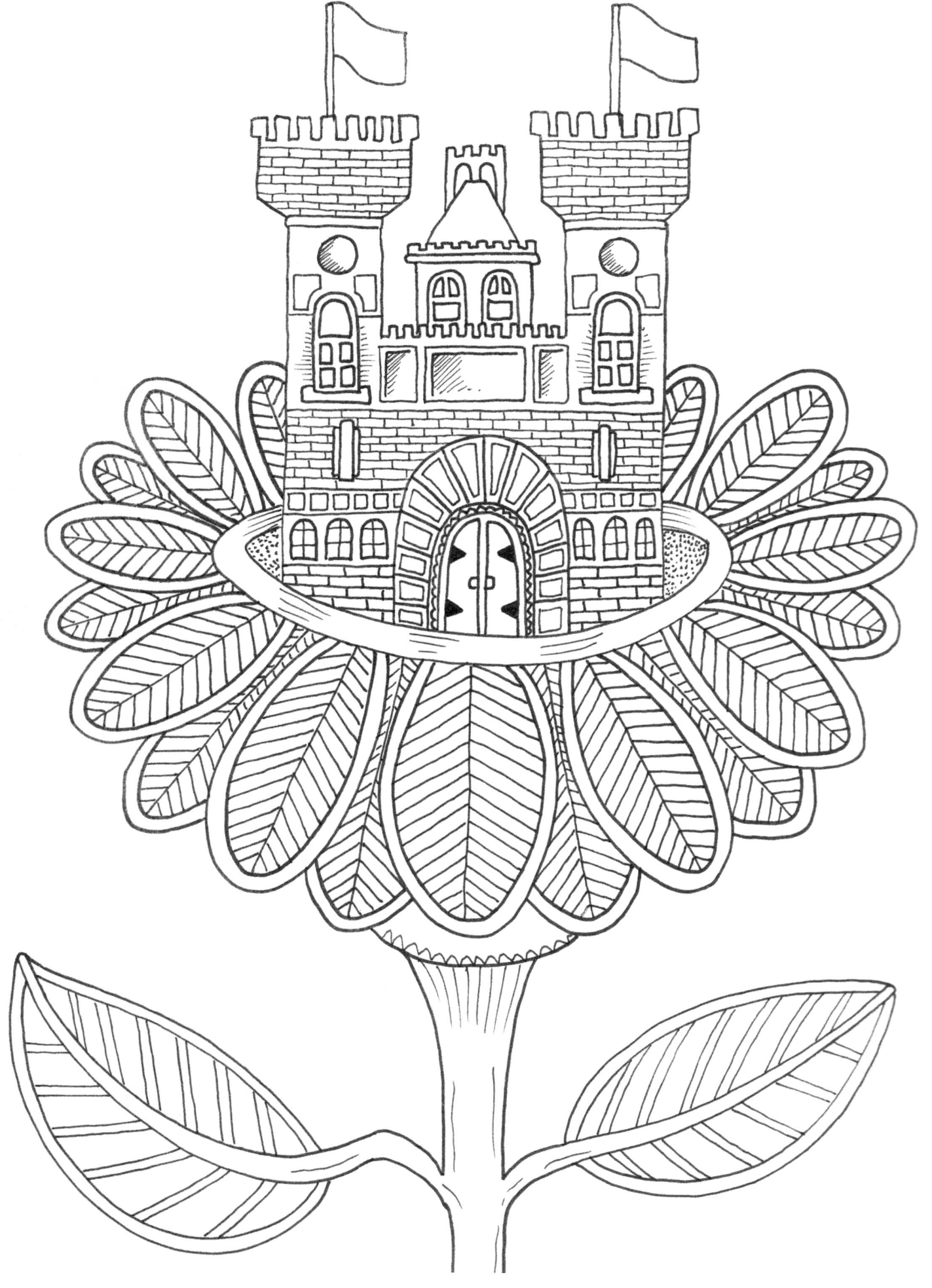

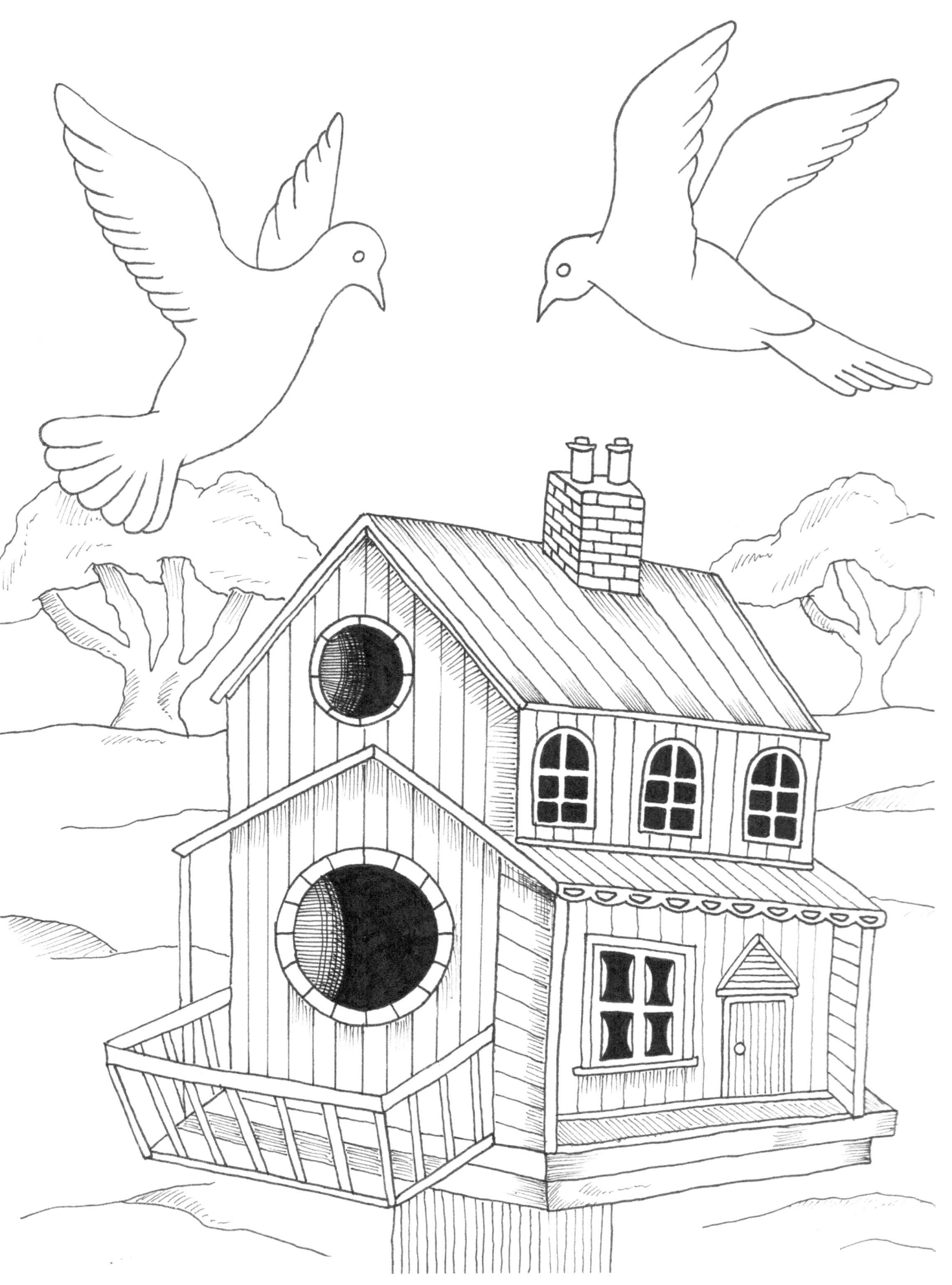

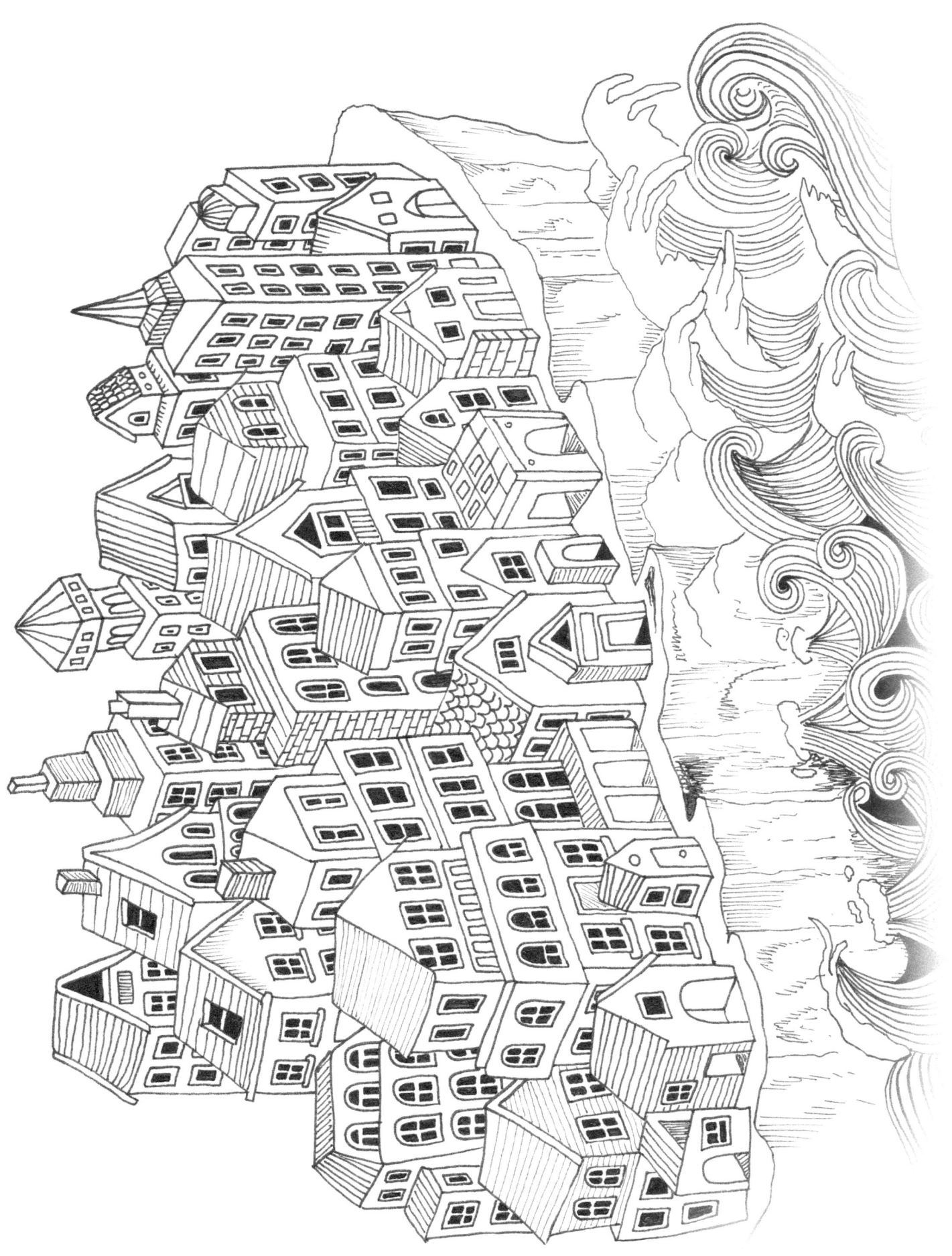

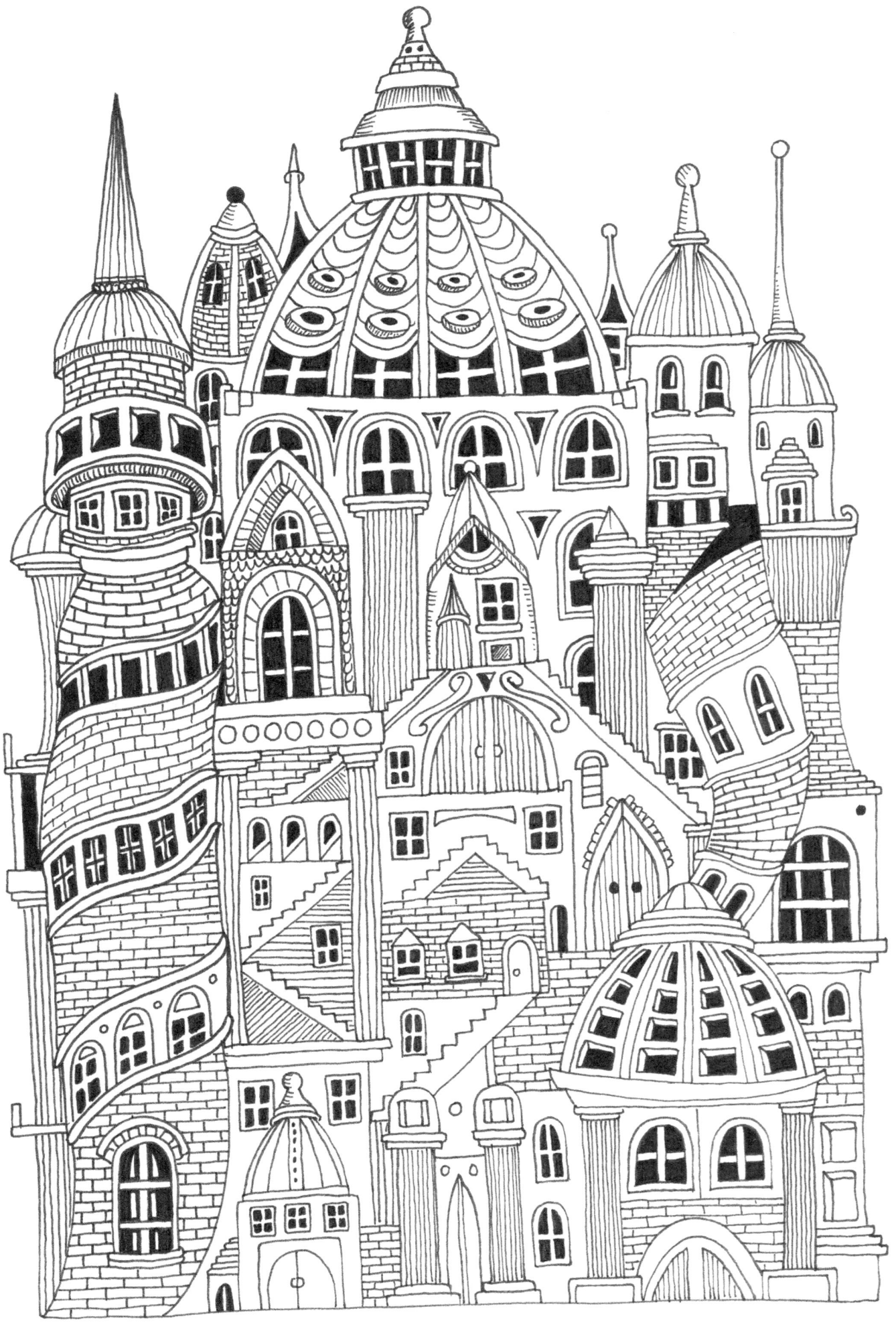

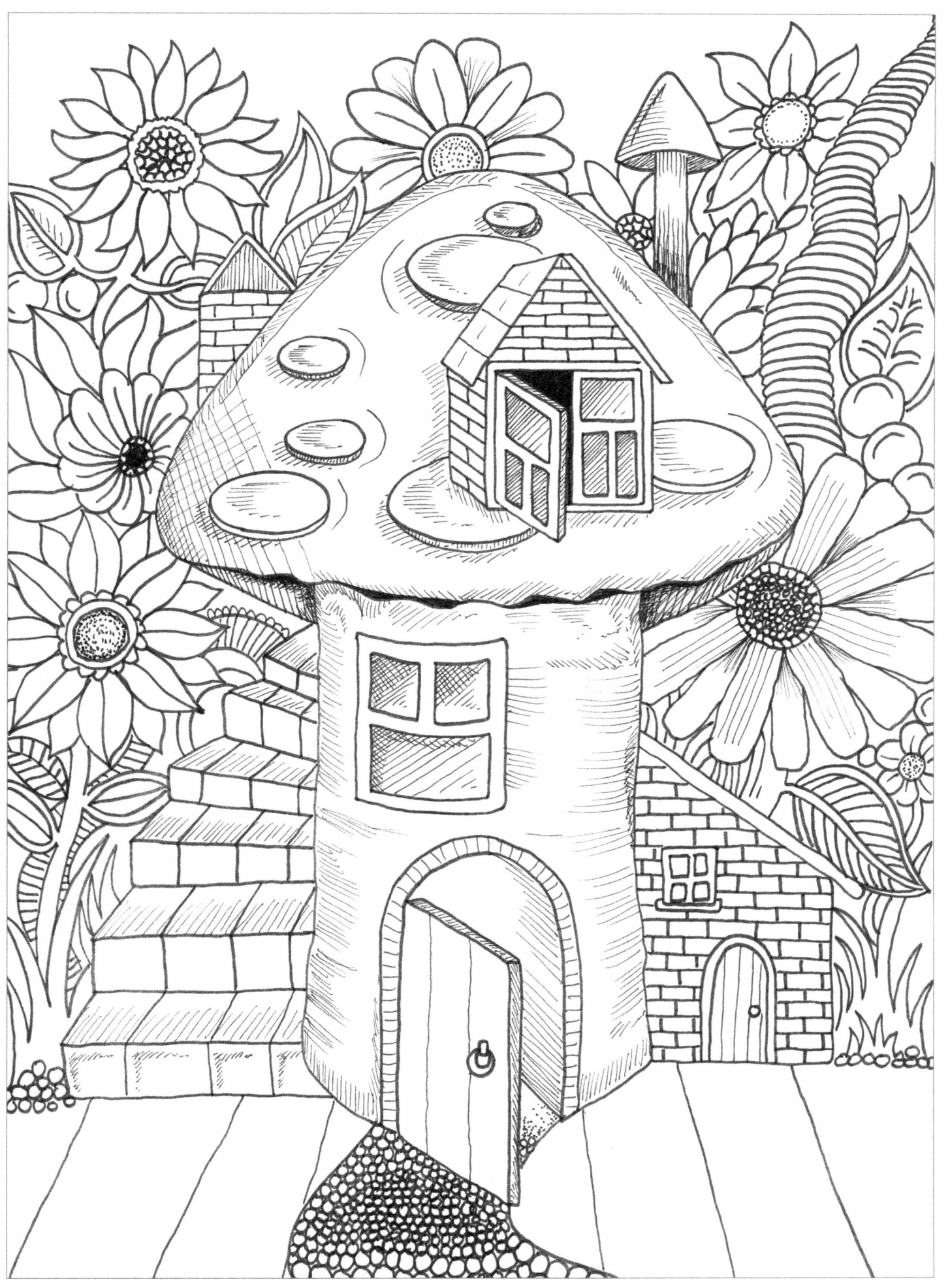

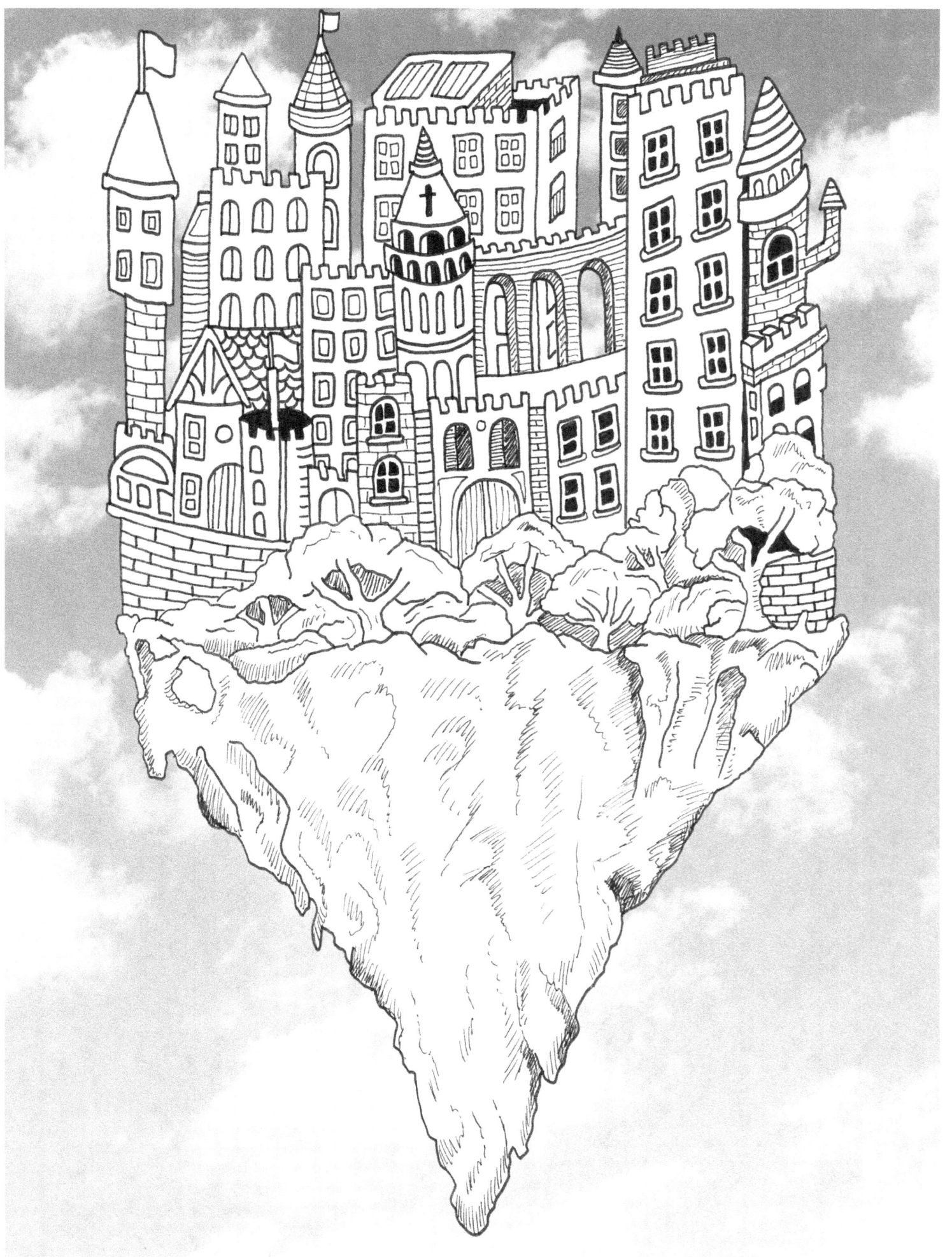

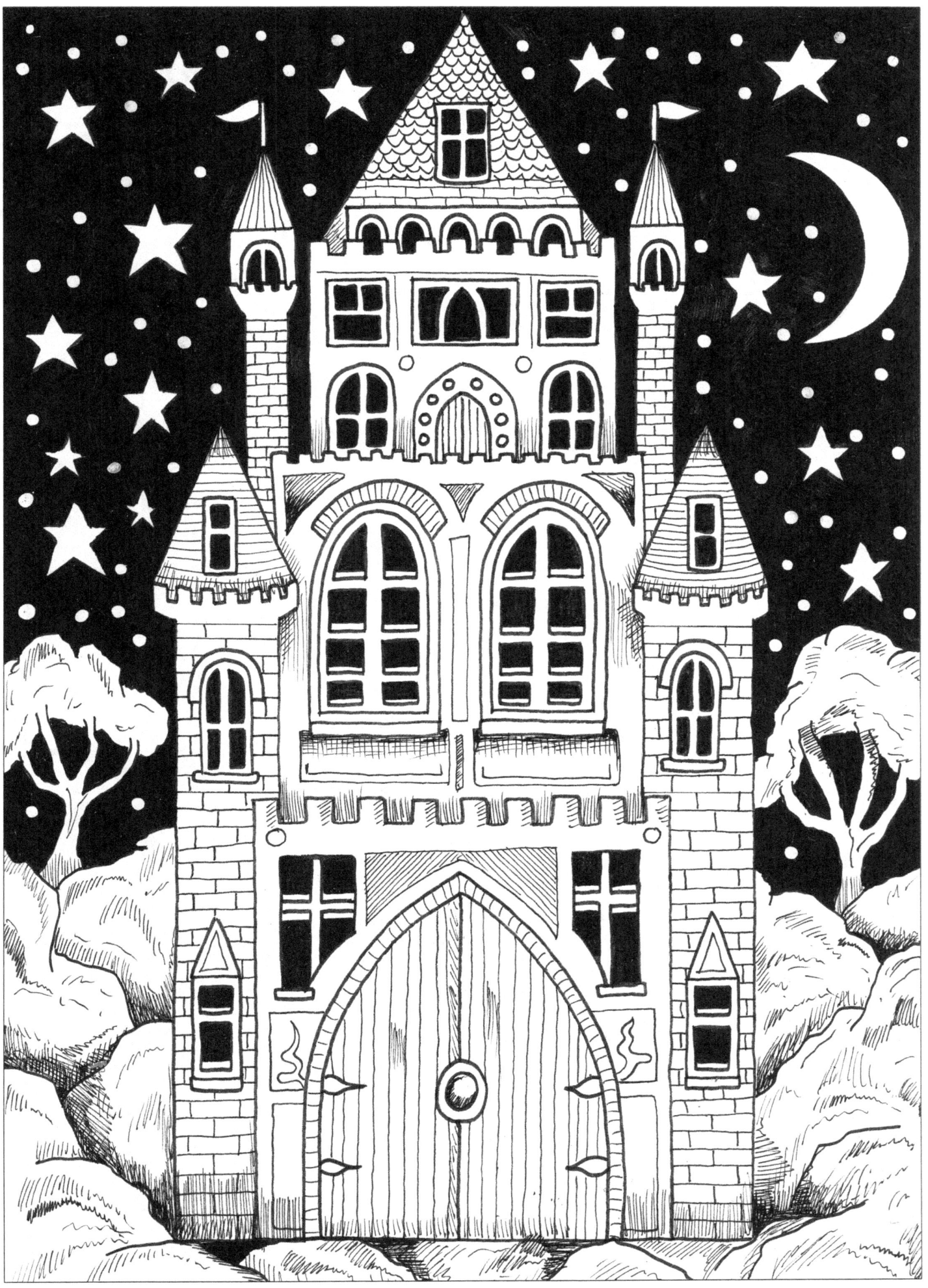

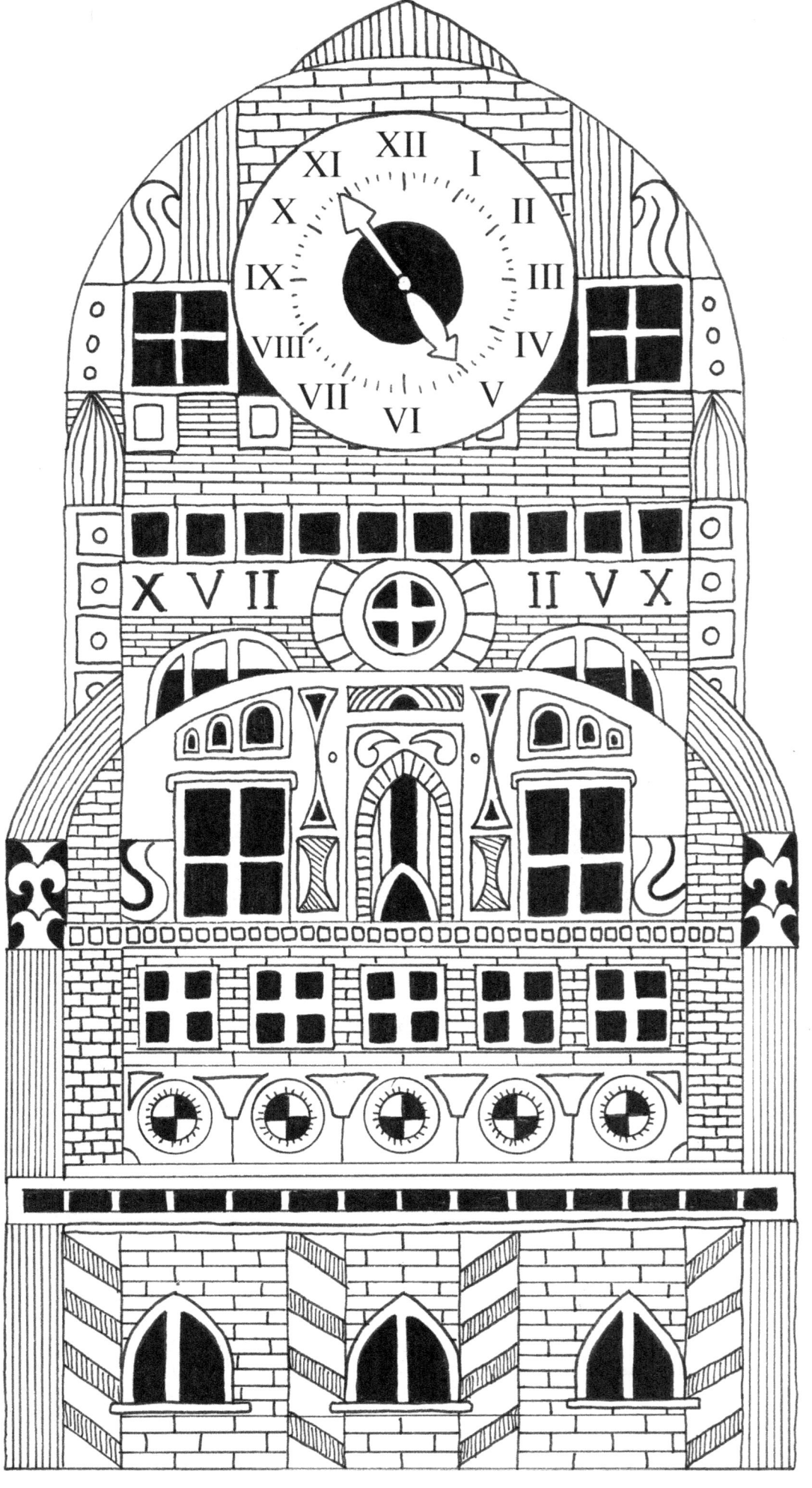

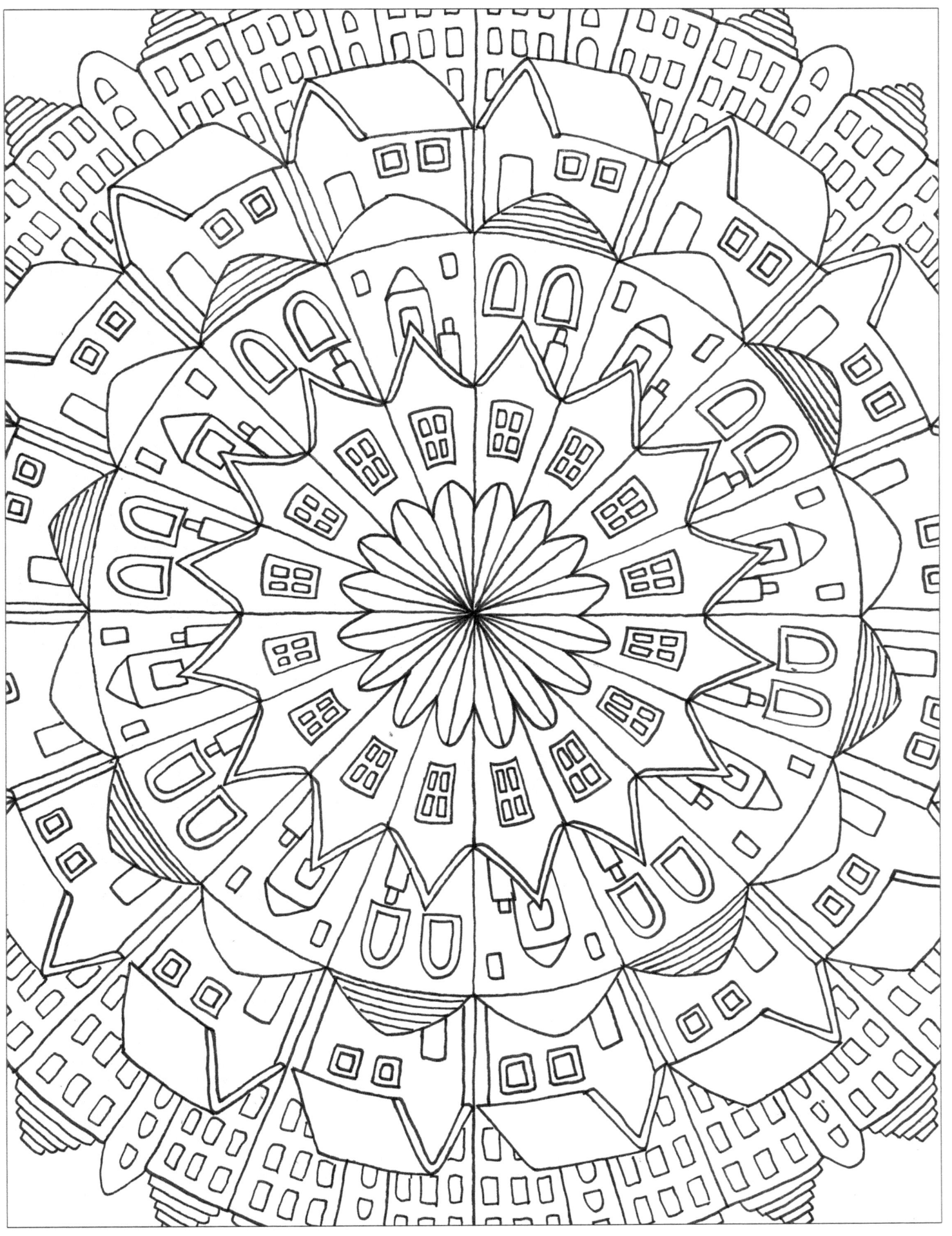

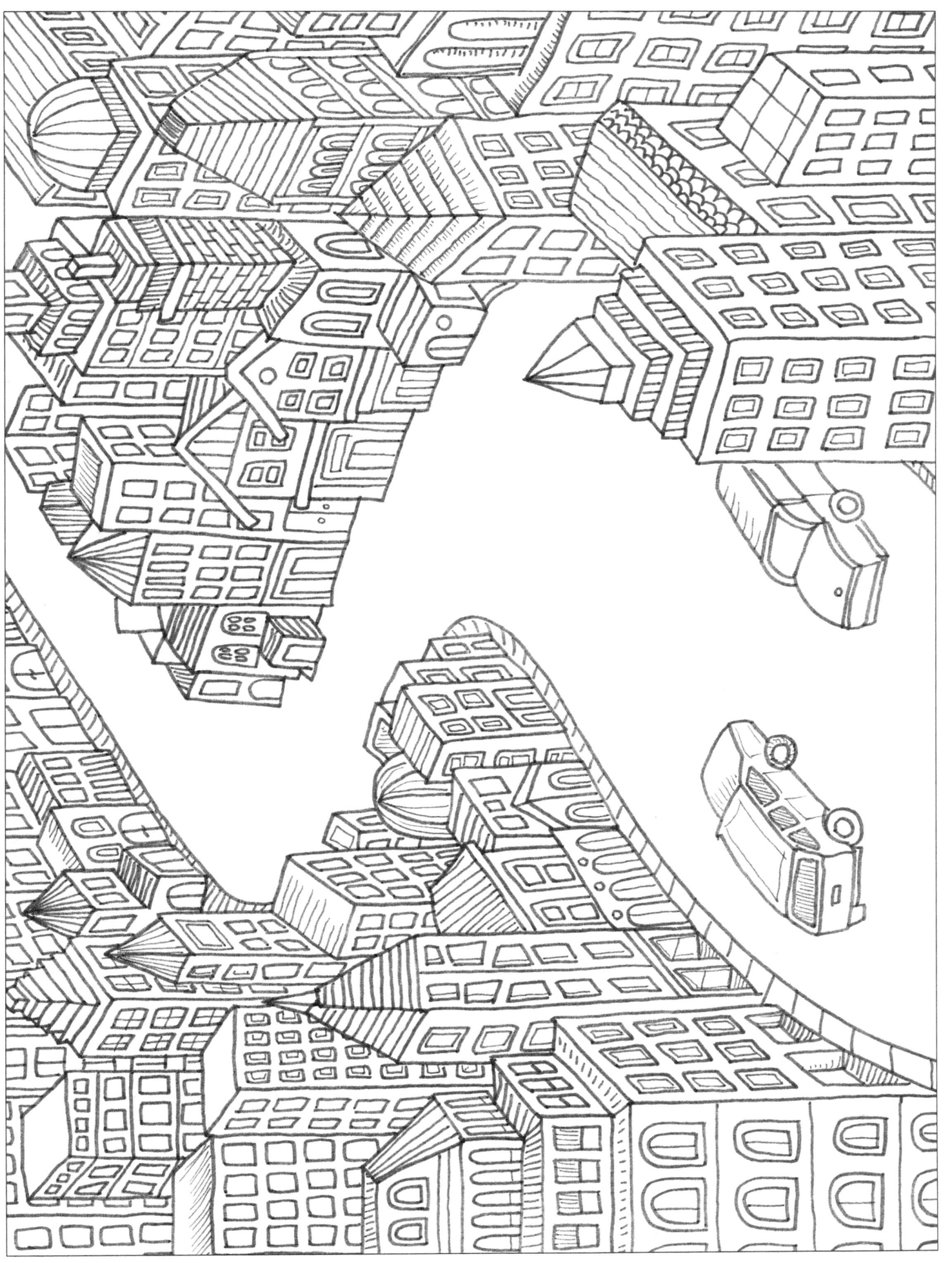

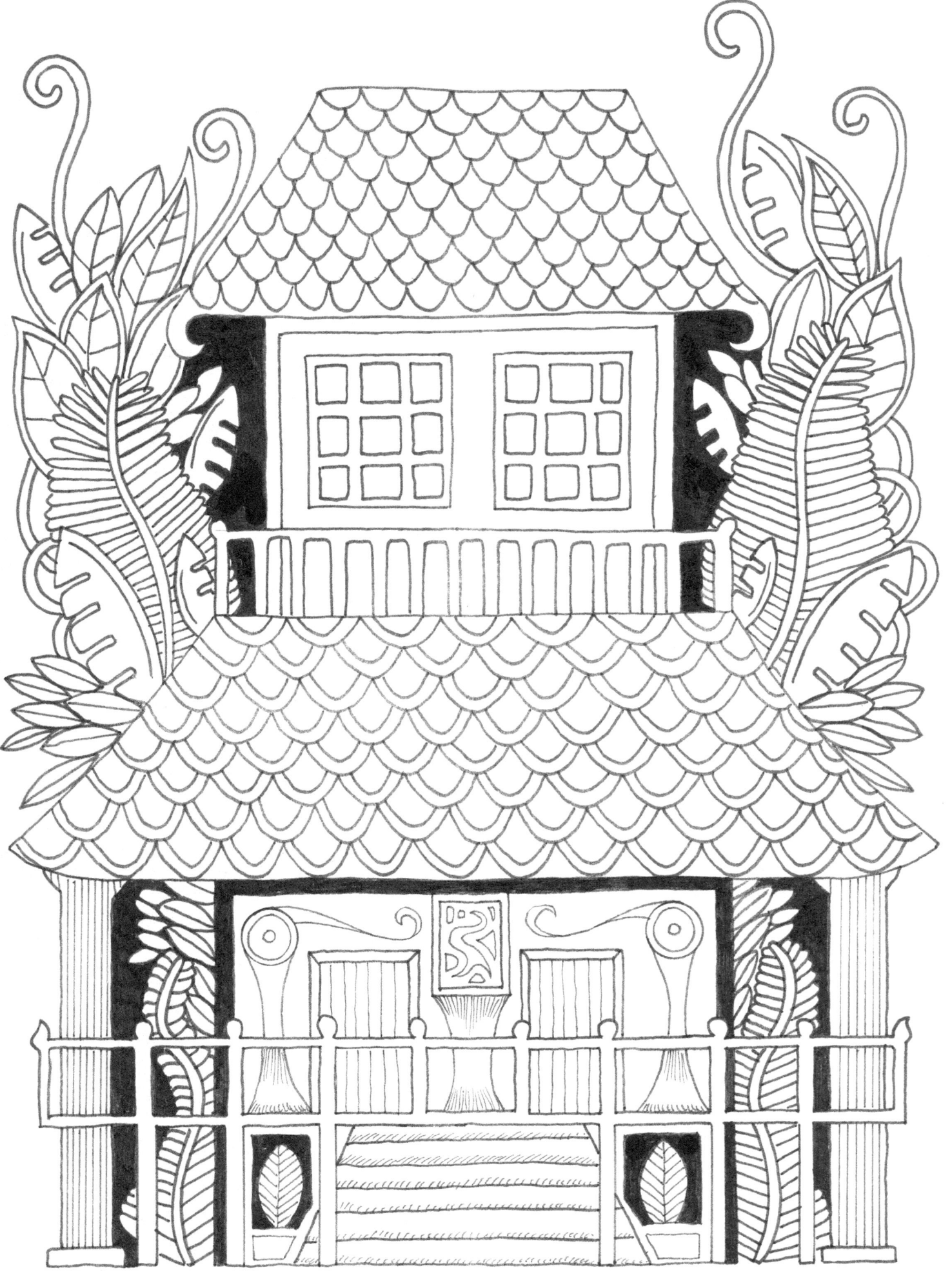

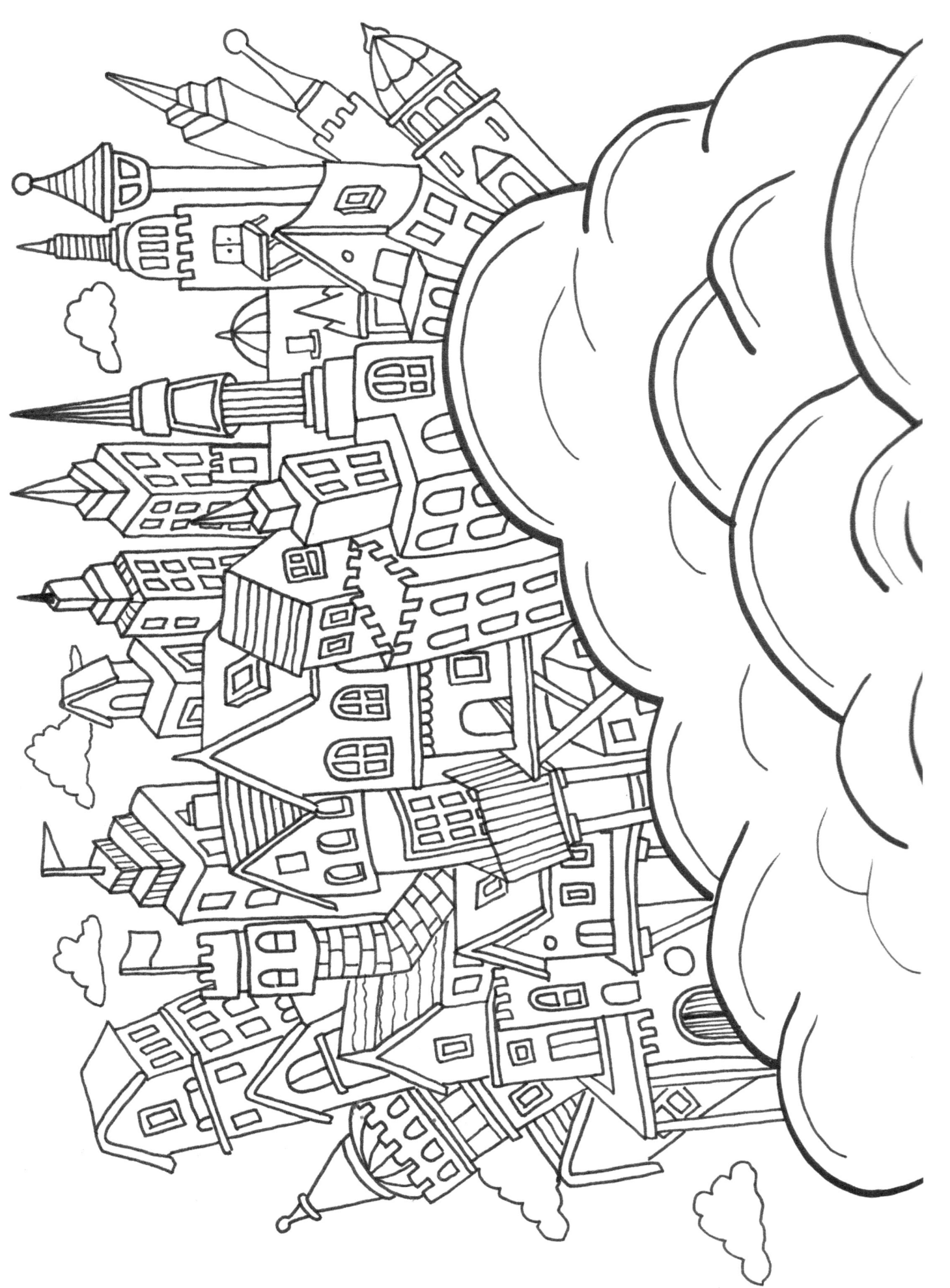

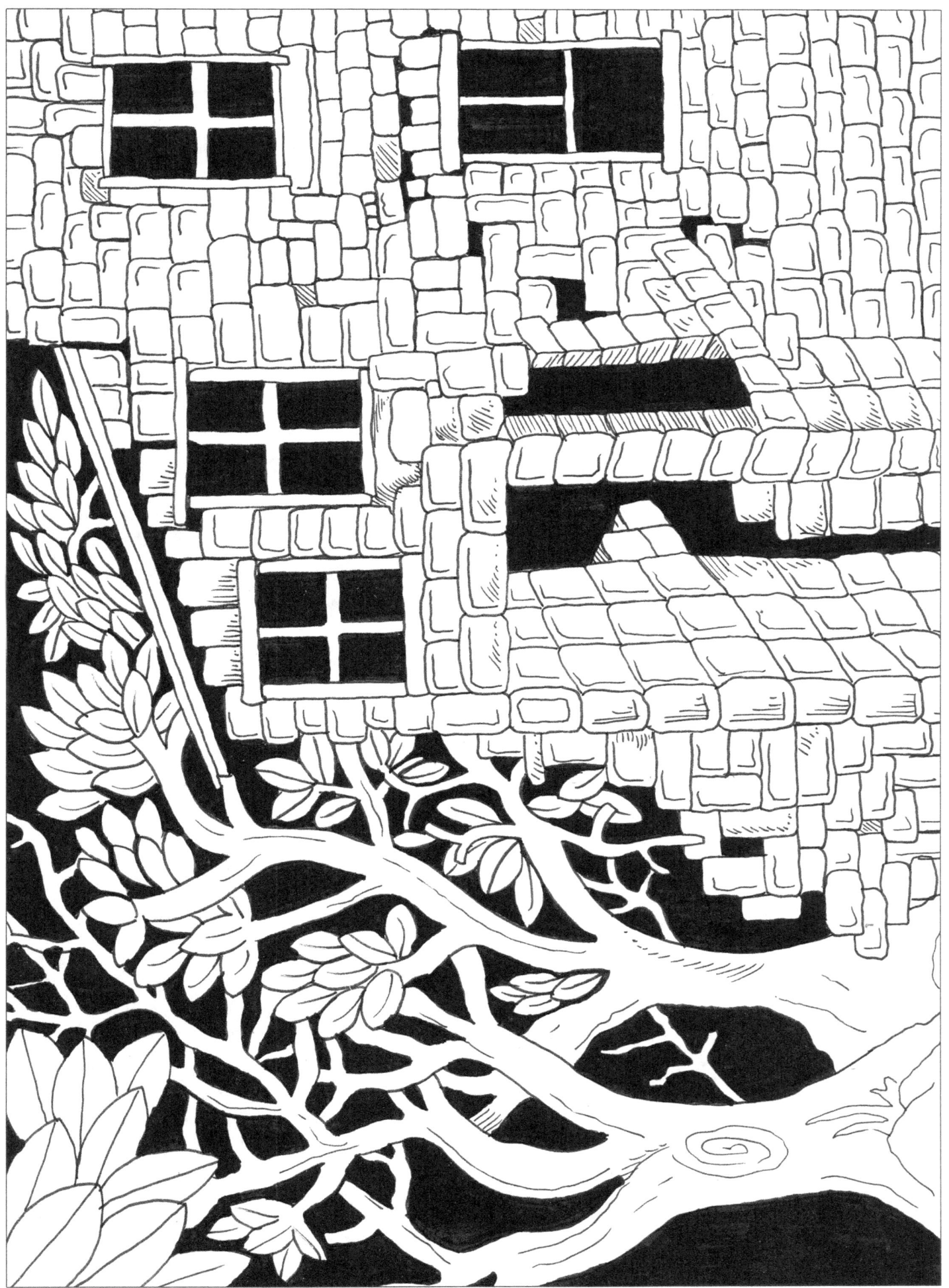

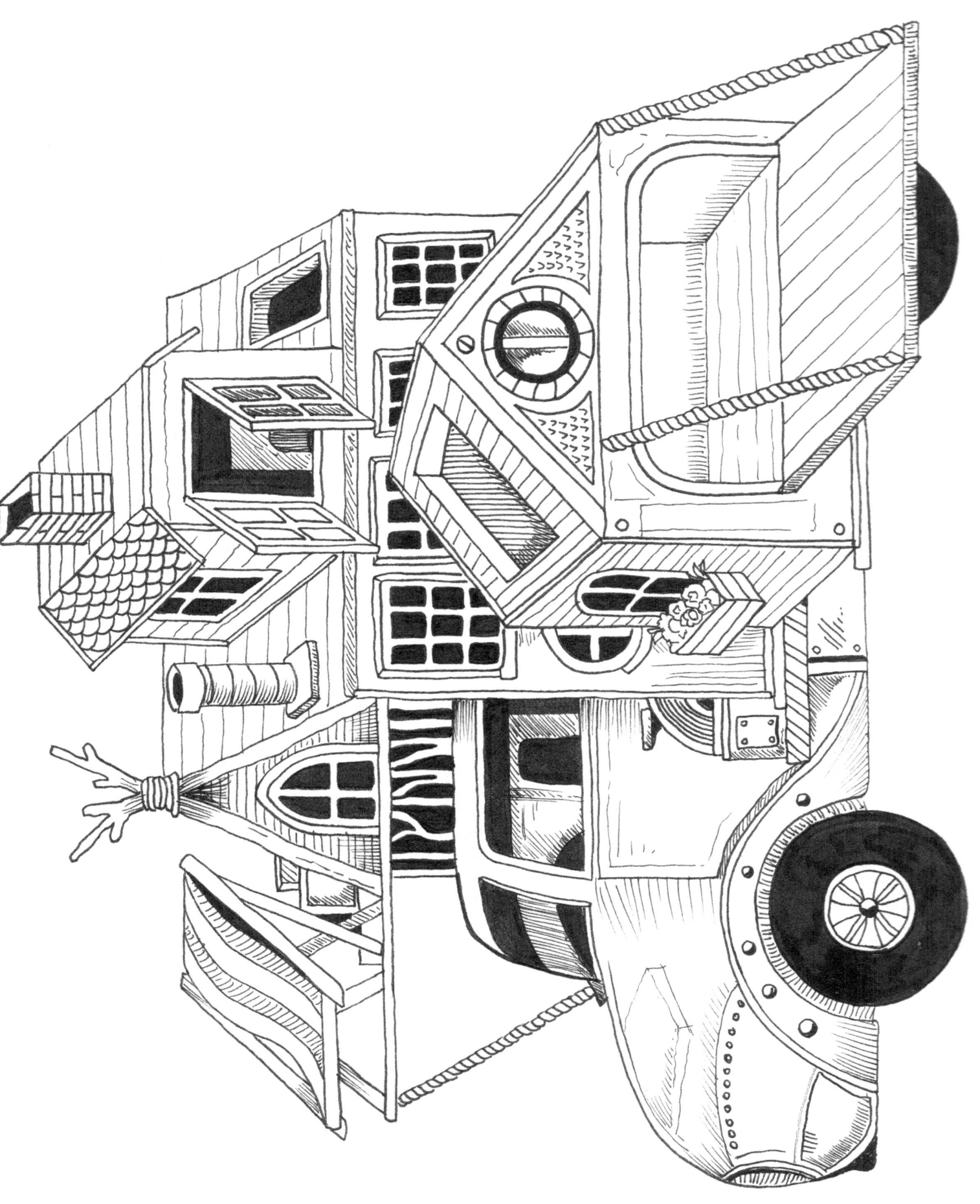

Imaginary Buildings
and Magical Lands

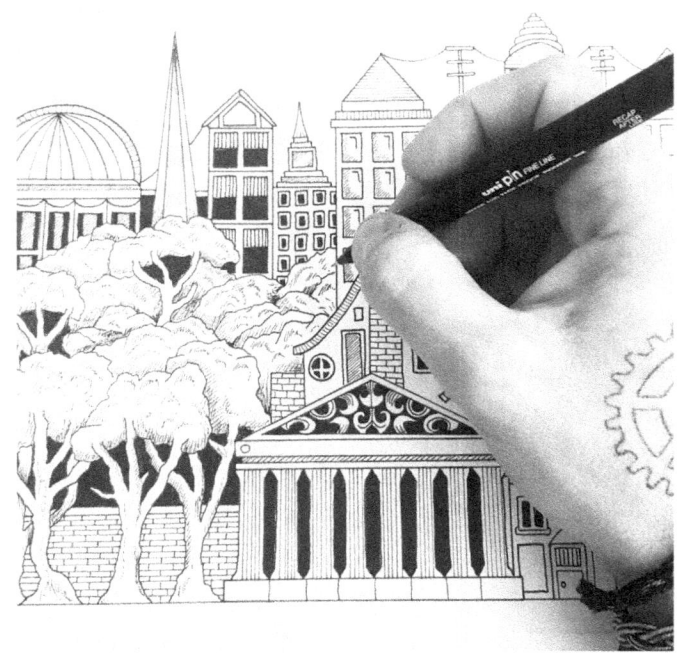

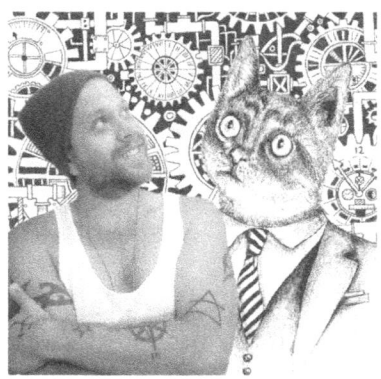

Yo! Thanks for buying my book! I really hope you enjoy colouring it as much as I enjoyed drawing it. Ever since I was a little boy I've always doodled cities. When you're young it's one of the easiest ways to get into art. You just do a ton of little boxes and add the windows... throw in some skyscrapers, old fashioned tiled roofs... the odd tree here and there. I guess this book is a throwback to my childhood!

On the left you'll see some progress shots of how a book like this comes to life. All my pictures are hand drawn – in the old fashioned way... with pens and pencils!

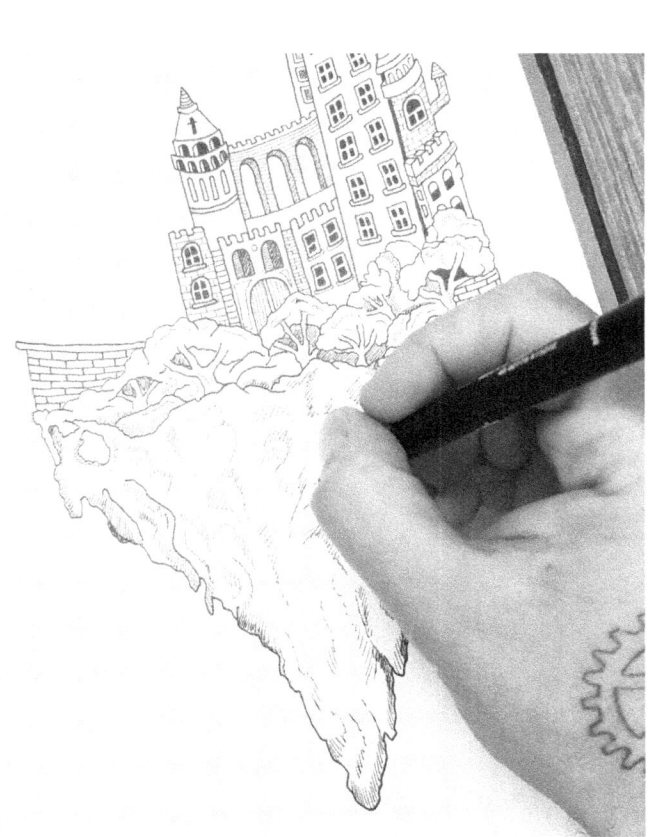

As with all my books, there are a load of people I'd like to thank for their support and advice in helping me bring this book to life. First and foremost, my wife Corina who not only puts up with me silently drawing most evenings, but also acts as an advisor and clean–up artist for the rough drawings. I'd like to thank my good friends Laura and Taylor for giving me some excellent ideas and support. On my facebook page, loads of you gave me brilliant ideas: Maria Husk, Marcia Bogaert, Debbie Beacom, Sharni Copham, Lee Jones, Karen Amoudry, Vicki Rhodes, Athena McNeill, Clare Sparkes and so many more. Thank you all so much for your continued support and ideas.

Lastly, as always, this book is dedicated to two little people. My biggest fans. To my beautiful daughters Poppy and Lola, this one is for you girls. I hope you never get bored of my drawings.

SQUIDOODLE
XXX

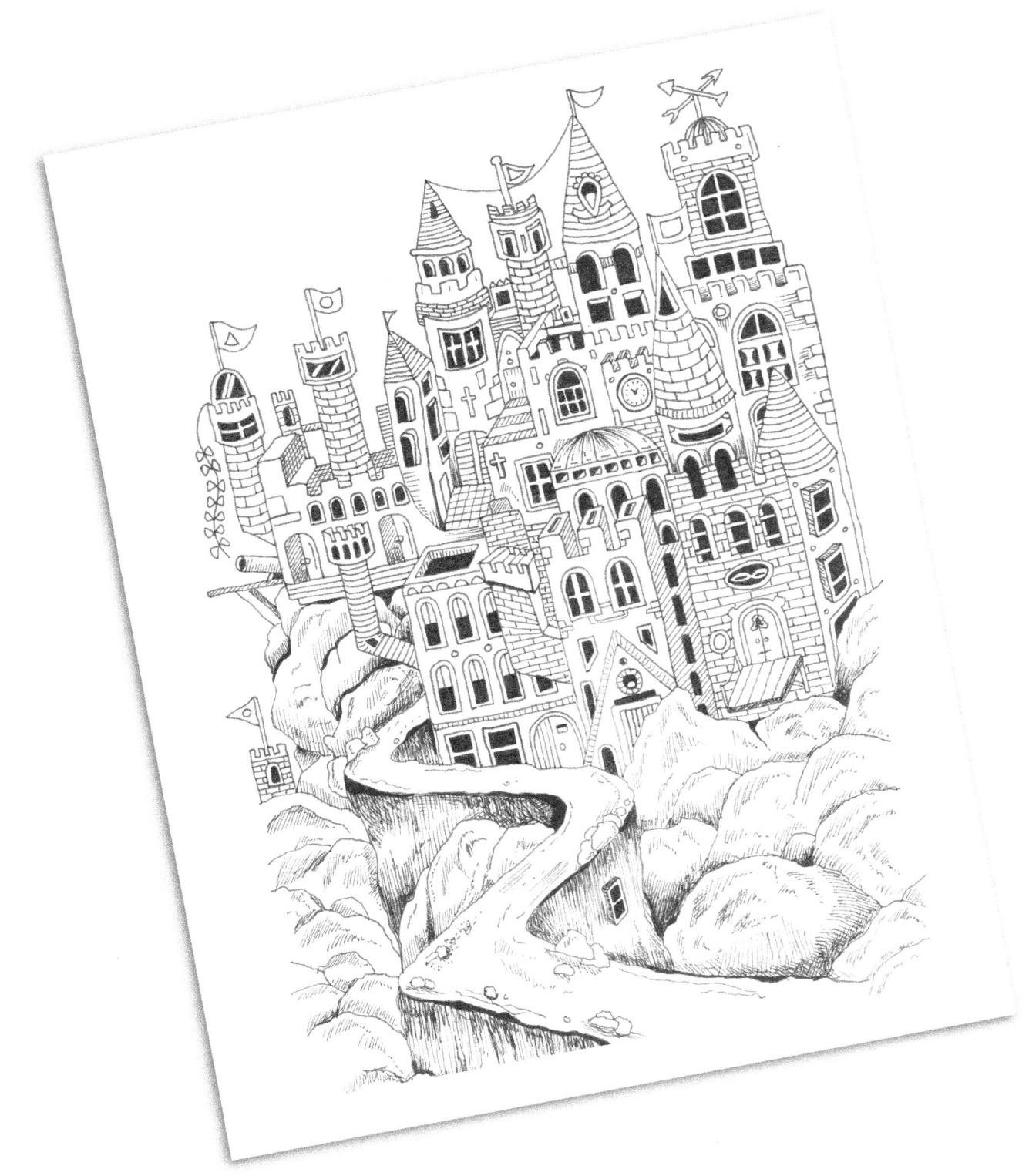

FREE DOWNLOAD!!! You can download "Fortress Doodle" from this book by visiting my website www.squidoodleshop.com alongside many other free pages! Whilst you're there, sign up for regular special offers and rambling newsletters.

...other Squidoodle coloring books available

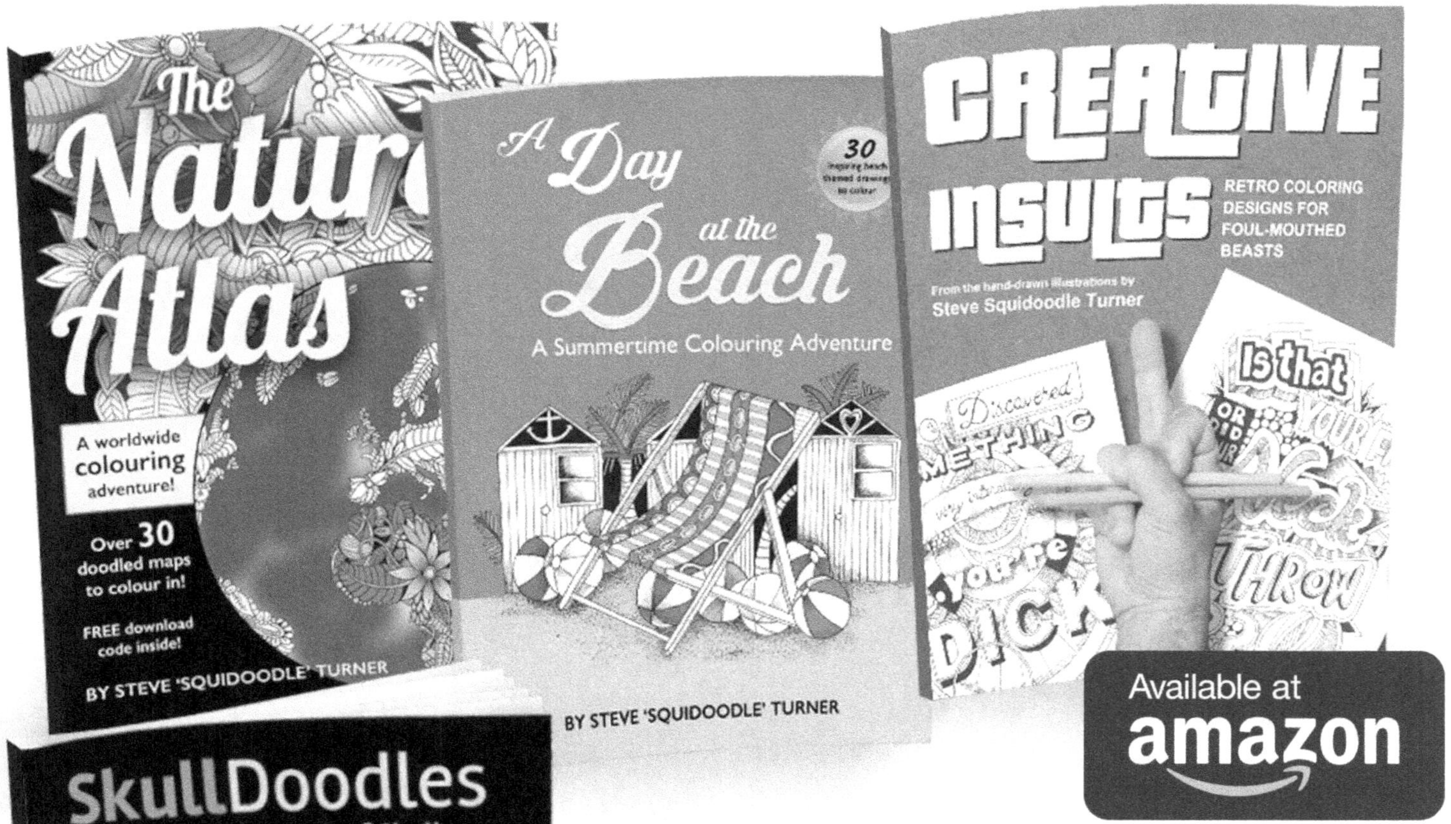

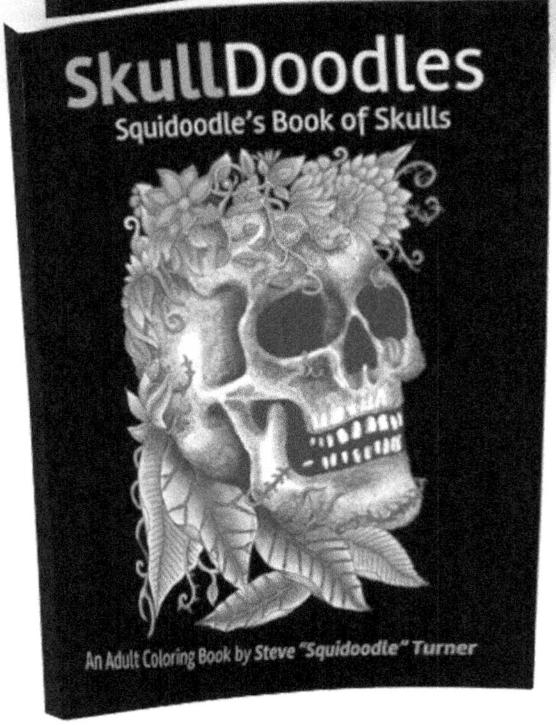

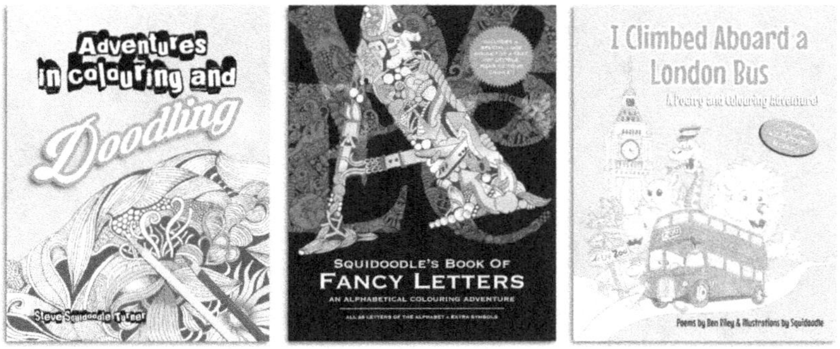

The Nature Atlas
A worldwide colouring adventure!
Over 30 doodled maps to colour in!
FREE download code inside!
BY STEVE 'SQUIDOODLE' TURNER

A Day at the Beach
A Summertime Colouring Adventure
30 inspiring beach themed drawings to colour
BY STEVE 'SQUIDOODLE' TURNER

CREATIVE INSULTS
RETRO COLORING DESIGNS FOR FOUL-MOUTHED BEASTS
From the hand-drawn illustrations by Steve Squidoodle Turner

SkullDoodles
Squidoodle's Book of Skulls
An Adult Coloring Book by Steve "Squidoodle" Turner

Adventures in colouring and Doodling
Steve Squidoodle Turner

SQUIDOODLE'S BOOK OF FANCY LETTERS
AN ALPHABETICAL COLOURING ADVENTURE
ALL 26 LETTERS OF THE ALPHABET + EXTRA SYMBOLS

I Climbed Aboard a London Bus
A Poetry and Colouring Adventure
Poems by Ben Xley & Illustrations by Squidoodle

All of my books are available to buy on Amazon.
Simply search for "squidoodle"

For original artwork, prints, greetings cards and **FREE** downloads, visit www.SquidoodleShop.com

 Get in touch! www.facebook.com/SquidDoodleArt